The Lives of
THE PROPHETS

The Lives of
THE PROPHETS

Leila Azzam

Illustrated by Khalid Seydo

HUD HUD BOOKS

Copyright © Hud Hud Books 1995

Hud Hud Books
Salisbury House
Station Road
Cambridge CB1 2LA

British Library Cataloguing-in-Publication Data
A catalogue record for this book is available from the British Library.

ISBN 1-900251-00-0 paper

No part of this book may be reproduced
in any form without prior permission of
the publishers. All rights reserved.

Designed and Pageset by CW Typographics
Origination by Walden Litho
Printed and bound in Italy

PREFACE

FROM ADAM ﷺ the first prophet to Muḥammad ﷺ the last messenger of God, there were many prophets but only one message; man should worship God and God alone. It was a message oft-repeated and oft-forgotten and the prophets sent by God to preach this message were more frequently met with chastisement than by support.

This book narrates the lives of the prophets for children and young adults and relates the severe trials and tribulations as well as the love and mercy which each prophet encountered from his own people in preaching their message. The main source for this book is the Holy Qur'ān which in the case of certain prophets, and the story of Joseph in particular, reveals considerable details, while with other prophets there is only a passing reference. For this reason I have also gone back to the Qur'ānic commentaries as well as the early Islamic sources. Since the book is largely aimed at a young readership, the translation of the Qur'ānic verses has been simplified. I have largely relied on the Yusuf Ali translation.

It is important to make clear that not all the prophets are mentioned in this book, for the Qur'ān tells us that there are many that we have not been told about, nor are the lives of those mentioned complete, in that the primary aim was to relate their lives as examples in piety, perseverance and patience for mankind.

The use of the traditional salutation for the prophets ﷺ[1] and for the prophet Muḥammad ﷺ[2] have been used only at the beginning of each chapter.

LEILA AZZAM

[1] Peace be upon him.
[2] The blessings and Peace of God be upon him.

ENGLISH/ARABIC NAME EQUIVALENTS

Aaron	Hārūn
Abraham	Ibrāhīm
Adam	Ādam
David	Dāwūd
Enoch	Idrīs
Imran	ʿImrān
Ishmael	Ismāʿīl
Isaac	Isḥāq
Jacob	Yaʿqūb
Jesus	ʿĪsā
Job	Ayyūb
John	Yaḥyā
Jonah	Yūnus
Joseph	Yūsuf
Lot	Lūṭ
Moses	Mūsā
Noah	Nūḥ
Samuel	Ṣamūʾīl
Saul	Ṭālūt
Solomon	Sulaymān
Zachariah	Zakariyya

CONTENTS

Preface	V
English/Arabic Name Equivalents	VI

ADAM ﷺ & CREATION	1
ENOCH ﷺ & THE ANGEL	6
NOAH ﷺ & THE ARK	9
HUD ﷺ & SALIH ﷺ	14
ABRAHAM ﷺ & THE KAʿBA	22
JOSEPH ﷺ & HIS DREAM	29
MOSES ﷺ & THE PHARAOH	36
DAVID ﷺ & SOLOMON ﷺ	47
JOB ﷺ & HIS PATIENCE	58
JONAH ﷺ & THE WHALE	62
ZACHARIAH ﷺ & JOHN ﷺ	65
JESUS ﷺ & HIS MIRACLES	69
MUHAMMAD ﷺ THE FINAL PROPHET	77

VIII

ADAM ﷻ & CREATION

GOD WAS a hidden treasure, He desired to be known, so He created the universe, full of galaxies, planets, moons and stars moving in harmony, all to praise Him. God created the angels from light and pure faith to praise Him. He created the *jinn* from fire and made a world for them to live in, so that they too can praise Him. He created the earth to circle around the sun so that there may be night and day and that there may be four different seasons.

> *And a Sign for them is the Night; We withdraw from it the Day, and behold they are plunged into darkness. And the Sun runs its course for a period determined for it; that is the decree of Him the Exalted in Might, the All-Knowing. And the Moon, We have measured for it stages to cross it till it returns like the old and withered lower part of a date-stalk.*
>
> (36:37-39)

Finally, God created the form of man out of clay. God blew His Spirit into the form of man and Adam, father of mankind, came to life.

> *He fashioned him in due proportion and breathed into him something of His spirit. And He gave you hearing and sight and feeling and understanding.* (32:9)

God bestowed many gifts upon Adam. He gave him the gift of sight so that he may marvel at the creation of God, and the senses of hearing, smell, taste and touch to help him appreciate and understand the universe around him. But that was not all that God bestowed upon Adam. God gave Adam two unique gifts: an intelligence which is able to tell what is right from what is wrong, and a will which is capable of doing what is good and refraining from what is evil. So while other creatures also possessed the senses, only Adam had the ability to know and the ability to choose. God then taught Adam the names of all things; and with these gifts He made him the perfect man and placed him above the angels.

Once Adam had mastered all the names, God decided to test the angels. God asked the angels,

> *'Tell Me the names of these if you do know.' They said, 'Glory be to You, of knowledge we have none, save what You have taught us, in truth it is You who are perfect in knowledge and wisdom.' He said, 'O Adam! tell them their names.' When he had told them, God said, 'Did I not tell you that I know the secrets of heaven and earth, and I know what you reveal and what you conceal?' (2:31-33)*

Then God commanded the angels to fall down in prostration before Adam as a sign of respect for his wisdom. All prostrated themselves. Now among the angels was a *jinn* who had been raised to the level of the angels because of his great virtue; his name was Satan. When God commanded the angels to prostrate themselves to Adam, He had included Satan in His command. But Satan refused. His answer was, "Why should I, Satan, a being of fire, humble myself before Adam who You have created from mere clay?" With this rebellion Satan showed how pride can destroy great virtue.

> *We bade the angels bow down to Adam, and they bowed down; not so Satan; he refused to be among those who bow down. God said, 'What prevented you from bowing down when I commanded you?' He said, 'I am better than he; You created me from fire, and him from clay.' (7:11-12)*

God banished Satan from Heaven for his disobedience. But Satan in his pride swore vengeance upon Adam and all his descendants, and vowed that from that day on he would plot and scheme to lead man astray. God then warned Satan that a terrible punishment awaited him, and anyone who chose to follow him.

> *God said, 'Descend from here. It is not for you to be arrogant here; get out, for you are the meanest of creatures.' He said, 'Give me respite till the day*

*they are raised up.' God said, 'You are among those who have respite.'
He said, 'Because You have thrown me out, lo! I will lie in wait for them
on Your Straight Way. Then I will assault them from before them and
behind them, from their right and their left: nor will You find, in most of
them, gratitude for Your mercies.' God said, 'Get out from this, disgraced
and expelled. If any of them follow you,—hell will I fill with you all.'*

(7:13-18)

In the Garden of Paradise, Adam lived in perfect peace and happiness. He never knew hunger or thirst, heat or cold. He never suffered from fear or sadness or pain. All he saw was the dazzling beauty that surrounded him and all he ever heard were the angels praising God.

Adam was alone in the Garden of Paradise; God decided to give him a companion. So while Adam slept, He, from the same soul, created the very first woman, Eve, the mother of mankind. Adam now had a companion he could talk to, and someone with whom he could share his day. Together they lived in the peace and happiness which only God can give.

Now among the many trees in the Garden of Paradise was a tree which Adam and Eve were not allowed to touch. God had forbidden them to eat of its fruit in order to test the strength of their obedience to Him.

One day, true to his promise, Satan appeared whispering evil to Adam and Eve. He tried, in every possible way to tempt them to eat the fruit of the forbidden tree. He told them that the tree was the tree of eternal life, and that if they ate from it they would never grow old nor would they ever die.

'Your Lord only forbade you this tree, lest you should become angels or such beings as live for ever.' And he swore to them both that he was their sincere adviser. (7:20-21)

For days Adam thought only of the tree, and Satan was always there tempting him with his lies, bidding him to eat of its miraculous fruit. Then, all of a sudden, Adam faltered and gave in to Satan's whisperings. Going against what God had commanded, Adam put his hand out to the tree, plucked a fruit, ate some of it and gave Eve also to eat. They had scarcely finished eating the fruit, when they were filled with sorrow and remorse, feelings they had never experienced before, and they realized, for the very first time, that they were naked. Frantically, both began to tear off leaves from the tree to cover their bodies.

When they tasted of the tree their shame became manifest to them, and they began to sew together the leaves of the garden over their bodies. (7:22)

Seeing that Adam and Eve had disobeyed Him, God banished them from the Garden of Paradise and sent them down to earth. Adam and Eve left Paradise, feeling ashamed and profoundly regretting their disobedience of God's Command. This event became known as 'the Fall'.

Adam sincerely repented of his sin, and with much remorse asked God to forgive both him and Eve. He continuously repeated this prayer:

'Our Lord! We have wronged our own souls: if You forgive us not and bestow not upon us Your Mercy, we shall certainly be lost.' (7:23)

God saw that Adam and Eve were truly repentant, and He forgave them. But He decreed that they would not return immediately to Paradise but that they, and their descendants, would live on earth until the Day of Judgement.

It was not long before Adam learned about the hardships of life on earth. Hardest of all things for him, however, was his constant battle with Satan, who never ceased to try to tempt him into defying the Will of God. Lost was the bliss and innocence which he and Eve had enjoyed in the Garden of Paradise. Nor was there any way to regain it except by remaining ever-faithful to God.

But Adam also witnessed the beauty and perfect harmony of God's creation. He saw the sun rise and give life on earth and he saw it set so that man can rest from his toil. He saw the crescent grow to a full moon and disappear again, so that man can count the days and the months of the year. He saw the change of seasons, and watched the plants and the trees grow from seeds deep in the ground to provide food for man. He saw animals, each species living in its own kingdom, there to help man on earth. And finally, Adam realized that just as God had placed him above the angels in Paradise, He had now made him king on earth.

Adam and Eve lived for a long time. They had many children and grandchildren who eventually spread all over the earth. When Adam came to die, he summoned together all of his children so as to give them his last words of advice. He told them to obey God and to always be wary of Satan's tricks. Most importantly they had to be humble before the might of God, and to remember that, as representatives of God on earth, they should act nobly and honourably at all times.

His counsel given, Adam died, and his soul returned to God. It remained for his children to keep to his message and to put his last words of advice into practice.

❖

ENOCH ﷺ & THE ANGEL

From the many children of Adam, God chose Seth to be both the prophet and the ruler of his people, caring for their spiritual and material needs. And, although Seth's descendants continued to rule after his death, none of them was a prophet until Enoch. Enoch was gifted with great wisdom, knowledge and many skills. He was the first man to use a pen and taught his people the art of writing. He was the first to set down weights and measures, and to record the movement of the stars. Before Enoch's time people wore the skins of animals; he was the first to sew and wear woven clothing. When sewing Enoch would praise God with every stitch he made, and if ever he sewed a stitch and neglected to praise God with it, he would at once undo the stitch and sew it again this time with praise. Enoch was also the first man to take up weapons to fight for God, as there were some people alive at his time who had turned away from God and had begun to worship fire.

At the age of forty, God made Enoch his messenger. From that day on, Enoch divided his time into two: for three days of the week he preached to his people, urging them not to neglect God and counselling them to do good deeds, and for four days he devoted himself to the worship of God.

It is related that one day the Angel of Death appeared to Enoch disguised as a handsome man. "Who are you?" asked Enoch. "I am the Angel of Death," he replied. Enoch asked the angel whether he had come to take his soul. But the angel said that God had not commanded him to do so, and that he had been sent simply to be Enoch's companion. "If that is so," said Enoch, "and as you are the Angel of Death, I want you to show me the horrors of Hell." The angel was puzzled and alarmed, for he could do no such thing without the permission of God. Now, since Enoch was a pious

man and a prophet, God granted him his wish. God ordered the angel to accompany Enoch to the Gates of Hell, so that he may gaze upon it. What Enoch saw there, nearly made him faint; the screams of terror and despair, the fire, the torment and suffering. Enoch was then brought back to earth, shaken by what he had witnessed. He was so overcome that he could hardly eat or sleep.

Enoch remained in this state for some time. Then one day, he asked the Angel of Death to take him to the Gates of Paradise. Once again the angel told him that, unless God commanded him, he was unable to do so. And so the angel conveyed Enoch's request to God. God then commanded a tree from Paradise to lower one of its branches to earth so that Enoch could grasp hold of it and be brought to Paradise. The wonders that Enoch saw in

Paradise took his breath away, and at once peace and contentment descended upon his soul. Meanwhile, the Angel of Death was waiting at the Gates of Paradise. He asked Enoch to come out of Paradise so that he could return him to earth. Enoch however refused; for having seen Paradise, he had no intention of returning to earth. "O Lord," said the Angel of Death, "what must I do? You have not given me permission to enter Paradise, and Enoch will not come out." God ordered the angel to leave Enoch in Paradise, and not to trouble him further, for out of His Mercy and Love, He could not ask Enoch to leave once he had entered Paradise. And so, with God's permission, Enoch remained in Paradise. God said of Enoch in the Qur'ān,

Also mention in the Book Enoch; for he was a man of truth, and a prophet and We raised him to a lofty station. (19:56-57)

NOAH ﷺ & THE ARK

For many generations, the descendants of Adam continued to follow his teachings, worshipping God alone. Among them were many brave and pious men, greatly loved and respected by their communities. Indeed the enormous grief felt by some people upon the death of their elders prompted them to make statues of these people so that no-one would forget them. Gradually, however, people forgot what the statues were for and began to worship them. In this way Satan succeeded in introducing the worship of idols among the descendants of Adam.

God always wants to guide people to what is true and good, and when He saw that one of the tribes had begun to worship idols, He decided to send them a prophet to guide them back to the true religion. God chose from among that tribe a man called Noah. Noah was neither a leader of his tribe nor a rich man, but he worshipped God faithfully and was, as the Qur'ān states, *'a grateful servant'*. (17:3)

Noah praised God continuously for blessings, great and small, and he urged his people to do the same. He also pleaded with his tribe to abandon the worship of idols, warning them that the wrath of God was terrible and His punishment severe.

> *We sent Noah to his people, and he said, 'O my people! Serve God. You have no other God save Him. Lo! I fear for you the retribution of an Awful Day.'* (7:59)

Now, although some of the poorer members of Noah's tribe were moved by his words and turned to God, the wealthy and powerful members of the tribe refused to listen to him. They would say to Noah, "Why did God choose to send His message through a man and not through an angel?" Noah would patiently reply that men not angels lived on earth, and that God had chosen him as a man who lived among them and who knew them all to convey to them His message. Then they would object that Noah's followers were poor and of low standing, and that it was unbecoming for them to associate with the poor. Noah replied that his followers had done nothing wrong, and that he could not reject them just because they were poor. God had sent him as a guide to all people, rich and poor alike. When they ran out of arguments, the idol-worshippers cursed Noah and accused him of madness.

> *The chieftains of his people said, 'Lo! we see you are in plain error.' He said, 'O my people! There is no error in me, but I am a messenger from the Lord of the Worlds. I convey to you the messages of my Lord and give good counsel to you, and know from God that which you know not. Do you marvel that there should come to you a Reminder from your Lord by means of a man among you, that he may warn you, and that you may keep from evil, and that haply you may find mercy.' But they denied him.*
>
> (7:60-64)

In Noah's time, people lived for much longer than people do today. Noah himself lived to be a thousand years old, and throughout his life he continued to preach patiently to his tribe, urging them not to stray from the path of God and warning of severe punishment for those who did. Noah's warnings, however, were to no avail, as most of his people would not believe him. Then one day, Noah received a message from God,

> *'None of your People will believe except those who have believed already.'*
>
> (11:36)

Saddened that his efforts had been in vain, Noah asked God to punish the idol-worshippers. Thereupon, God decreed that a terrible flood would cover the whole earth, and He ordered Noah to build an ark which would save him from this calamity. Ever obedient to God, Noah went out in search of material with which to build his ark. But in the land where Noah lived, there were no forests and no wood with which to build an ark. So Noah had to plant trees and wait for them to grow.

When the trees had grown, Noah set to work building his ark. The idol-worshippers, seeing him at his work, laughed at him and mocked him. Surely Noah was mad, for only a madman would build an ark far away from any sea or river. Although he was now quite old, Noah continued to work tirelessly until, at last, the ark was completed. God ordered Noah to take on board the ark a male and a female from every species of bird, reptile, insect and mammal. He was also to invite the believers to join him.

'Embark on the Ark, in the name of God, whether it move or be at rest! For my Lord is, be sure, Oft-Forgiving, Most Merciful!' (11:41)

Only a few people joined Noah. Even his wife and one of his sons refused, not believing in what he prophesied. Then, in accordance with God's promise, it began to rain and rain. Gradually the valleys began to fill up with water. At this point, Noah again called to his son to believe in God and climb aboard the ark, but he appealed in vain.

And Noah called out to his son, who had separated himself from the rest, 'O my son! embark with us, and be not with the Unbelievers!' The son replied, 'I will go to a mountain; it will save me from the water.' Noah said, 'This day nothing can save from the Command of God any but those on whom He has mercy!' And the waves came between them, and the son was among those overwhelmed by the flood. (11:42-43)

The water kept rising and rising, springs gushed forth from the ground and rivers broke their banks, and still the disbelievers were blind to the danger. But soon it was too late, the flood submerged houses, trees and even the highest mountains and covered the whole earth. Everyone drowned save Noah and his followers, safe in the ark.

For a long time, the ark rode the mighty waves of what was now an ocean that stretched as far as anyone could see. Noah and his companions prayed God to keep them safe. Finally, God ordered the rain to stop and gradually the flood began to subside. From the ark, Noah sent out a dove to see if there was any land nearby. It was not long before the dove returned with an olive branch in its beak and traces of soil on its claws. Everyone rejoiced. Shortly afterwards, the ark came to rest upon Mount

Jūdī, where Noah and his companions disembarked and prostrated themselves to God in gratitude for having saved them.

> *Then the word went forth, 'O earth swallow up your water, and O sky withhold your rain.' And the water abated, and the matter was ended. The Ark rested on mount Jūdī, and the word went forth, 'Away with those who do wrong.'* (11:44)

The animals were then set loose and allowed to roam freely. Life on earth had begun once again. Noah continued to teach the right way to live, and the children of Adam returned to the original state in which God had created them, believing whole-heartedly in the One God.

HŪD ﷺ & ṢĀLIḤ ﷺ

THE DESCENDANTS of Noah and of the believers who had joined him in the ark spread all over the earth to repopulate it. The memory of the Flood and of how God in His mercy had saved mankind remained with people for many generations. Gradually, however, people began to forget the worship of God and became concerned solely with things in this world, even to the point of worshipping the physical things around them.

Now God is patient with mankind and wishes always to guide them to what is right. He sends His prophets to teach mankind the truth about their Lord and to instruct them in the correct ways of worship. Among the prophets that God sent to mankind after the flood were Hūd and Ṣāliḥ.

Hūd was a descendant of Shem, the son of Noah. He was born in the south of the Arabian peninsula to a tribe called ʿĀd. The land in which ʿĀd lived was very fertile, and thus the people were prosperous, living lives of luxury. They built palatial homes with gardens and fountains. ʿĀd were also famous for being strong in body and beautiful to look at. But instead of being grateful to God for all that He had granted them, ʿĀd were proud, harsh and cruel. They had given up worshipping God and were the first tribe after the Flood to worship idols.

ʿĀd had three idols which were housed together in a temple. Hūd's father was among those who served in the temple. But Hūd, even as a child, could not believe in the idols and, receiving direct guidance from God, worshipped Him alone. Hūd's mother, who was a pious woman and who had seen great visions at her son's birth, was the only person to encourage him in his worship.

When Hūd reached the age of forty, God revealed to him that he was the prophet of the tribe ʿĀd, and that he should preach to them the worship of the One God. So Hūd began to preach, saying to his people, "What are these stones that you worship. You carve them yourselves and then you turn to them for help; they can do you no good. There is only one God who deserves your worship. It is He who created you and who gave you all that you possess. Believe in God lest He punish you as He punished Noah's people."

The people of ʿĀd ridiculed Hūd and accused him of madness. But Hūd continued to preach to them, saying, "O my people, I am not insane. I have lived with you for many years and you know that there is nothing wrong with me. Is it so strange that God should choose one of you as a prophet? If you ask God for forgiveness and you worship Him sincerely, He will increase you in wealth and power. And after death, He will reward you with even greater goodness. But those who do not believe will be punished in this life and in the next."

Only a handful believed Hūd, the rest of ʿĀd refused to believe. In their pride, they said, "We outnumber you and your invisible God and are far stronger than He." Hūd warned his people that if they did not believe in God, He would punish them severely. But they only laughed, and mockingly asked Hūd to tell them exactly how God would punish them. Hūd did not give up hope and continued to preach to his people. In fact, he preached to them for seventy years, but to no avail.

God then sent ʿĀd a sign to warn them that their punishment was imminent. The tribe had once boasted to Hūd of their numbers. They had said, "One thousand baby boys are born to us each day, they will grow up to fight you and your God." But suddenly all the women of ʿĀd became barren and bore no children at all. Despite this warning from Heaven, ʿĀd only became more arrogant. Hūd then went out into the desert and prayed to God to send ʿĀd a second warning, and then, if they did not heed this second warning, to destroy them all.

God answered Hūd's prayer and instructed him to leave ʿĀd and to take with him all those who believed in God. God, then, caused a terrible drought to cover all the lands of ʿĀd and no rain fell for a long time. The fields started to shrivel up and the trees and the animals were all dying. But still ʿĀd would not believe.

Hūd returned once more to ʿĀd to warn them that worse was still to come, but also to give them hope in the mercy of God Who forgives all sins. Hūd told them that God would immediately bring back the rains and would make the country flourish again if only ʿĀd would believe.

But ʿĀd wanted to hear nothing of repentance, and so Hūd left them to their destiny. Soon thick black clouds could be seen on the horizon. The clouds drew closer and closer, and ʿĀd rejoiced thinking that the rains had finally come. But when the clouds reached ʿĀd, they enveloped the whole land in darkness. At the same time, a very strong wind started blowing as if from nowhere. The wind blew for seven days and seven nights. When it stopped, all the houses had been destroyed, all the gardens had been uprooted, and all the people were dead. ʿĀd was no more.

> *Then when they saw a cloud crossing the sky, coming to meet their valleys, they said, 'This cloud will give us rain.' No, it is the punishment you were eager to see, a wind in which is a grievous penalty. Everything it will destroy by the command of the Lord. Then by the morning, nothing was to be seen, but the ruins of their houses. Thus We recompense those given to sin.* (46:24-5)

Only Hūd and his followers were saved. Together they left the land of ʿĀd and settled in another area of the Arabian peninsula called Ḥaḍramūt.

> *And when Our sentence came to be put into execution, We delivered Hūd and those who had believed with him through Our Mercy.* (11:58)

Another of the prophets that God sent to mankind after the Flood was Ṣāliḥ. Ṣāliḥ was born to the tribe of Thamūd who lived in northern Arabia. This tribe was known for the beautiful houses that they carved in the sides of the mountains. Thamūd lived some time after the destruction of ʿĀd, but still within memory of the terrible punishment that befell them. Thamūd, however, no longer believed that what had happened to ʿĀd was a real event, and thought that it must just be a myth. Soon they took to worshipping idols, and in particular a large golden idol.

Ṣāliḥ's father was a pious man who believed in God and refused to worship the idol. He had had a vision that his son would one day be a prophet. When the King of Thamūd heard of this vision, he banished Ṣāliḥ's father from the land. So Ṣāliḥ lived alone with his mother and together they worshipped God.

Then one day, the archangel Gabriel came to Ṣāliḥ to tell him that God had chosen him as a prophet to Thamūd. Ṣāliḥ must show his tribe the error of their ways and must preach to them the correct worship of the One God. Now, Ṣāliḥ was known among his people for wisdom and goodness. Everyone in his tribe loved him. But when Ṣāliḥ started urging them to stop worshipping the idols and to worship God, they turned against him. They said,

> *'O Ṣāliḥ! You were one of us, centre of our hopes up till now. Do you now forbid us the worship of what our fathers worshipped? We are in great doubt as to that which you invite us to.'* (11:62)

Ṣāliḥ replied that he loved them and only wanted what was good for them. But Thamūd would not believe him, and scolded him for asking them to give up their idols.

In those days, people lived much longer than they do today. Ṣāliḥ went on preaching to his people year in year out. In fact, he preached to them for one hundred years, but only a few believed in his message.

Finally, Thamūd said to Ṣāliḥ, "We will only believe in you if you perform a miracle for us. We want you to bring forth a she-camel from the side of this mountain. She must be unlike any other she-camel in strength and beauty. She must give enough milk for the whole tribe to drink, and her milk must be cool in the summer and warm in the winter. She can drink from our well only every other day. She must also speak and bear witness that your God is one and true, and that you are sent to us from Him."

Ṣāliḥ said to them, "If God produces such a she-camel, will you finally believe in Him?" They said that they would. Ṣāliḥ had one condition, that no-one must ride the she-camel or harm her in any way. To this Thamūd agreed.

> *This she-camel of God is a sign to you. So leave her to graze in God's earth and let her come to no harm, or you shall be seized with a grievous punishment. (7:73)*

No sooner had they concluded the pact, when a mountain nearby shook and a rumble like thunder could be heard. From the mountain a she-camel appeared the likes of which no-one had ever seen. The she-camel stood in front of all of Thamūd and spoke, "There is no god save the One God, and Ṣāliḥ is the messenger of God." On seeing this, a large number of people believed, but an even larger number went against their promise to Ṣāliḥ and still would not believe in God.

The she-camel grazed in the mountains, and wherever she passed the trees would lower their branches so that she may eat. On the day that she was allowed to drink from the well, she would drink all the water. But in return she would give all the tribe to drink of her milk.

> *She shall have her portion of water, and you shall have your portion of water alternately, on a day appointed for you. (26:155)*

But there were some of Thamūd who were not pleased that Ṣāliḥ should be listened to, and wanted all the power for themselves. On seeing how people had begun to follow Ṣāliḥ after the miracle of the she-camel, they concluded that if the she-camel were no longer there, people would not follow Ṣāliḥ and would follow them. They decided to kill the she-camel.

On one of the days when the she-camel came to drink at the well, they were waiting for her and when she appeared they attacked her and killed her. When the news reached Ṣāliḥ and his followers that the she-camel was dead, they wept. God then told Ṣāliḥ to warn the unbelievers among Thamūd of a punishment from Him that will come upon them in three days time.

> *But they did kill her. So he said, 'Enjoy yourselves in your homes for three days, then will be your ruin, there is a true promise.' (11:65)*

God in His mercy gave Thamūd the three days as a chance for them to repent. But instead of repenting, Thamūd spent the three days plotting how they would kill Ṣāliḥ.

They said, 'We shall make a secret night-attack on him and his people, and we shall say to his heir, "we were not present at the slaughter of his people and we are telling the truth."' (27:49)

When the people woke on the morning of the fourth day, they found that fires were coming out of the ground and their houses started burning. Then fire started pouring down on them from the clouds in the sky. Finally, a terrible earthquake struck them and everything was destroyed.

God, however, protected Ṣāliḥ and his followers from the punishment that befell the rest of Thamūd. He led them to a different land where they lived in peace.

When Our decree issued, We saved Ṣāliḥ and those who believed with him by a grace from Ourselves. (11:66)

ABRAHAM ﷺ & THE KA'BA

MANY HUNDREDS of years after the Flood, the valley of the Euphrates was inhabited by a people who built a great empire. One of the rulers of this empire was a tyrant and his people lived in great fear of him. This nation had ceased to worship God and worshipped idols which were housed in huge temples and were guarded by powerful priests.

Abraham was born in a town situated in the southern part of the valley of the Euphrates. Abraham's father was one of the elders of his tribe, and commanded respect from everybody. He was a skilled craftsman and often carved the statues of the gods that the people worshipped.

Blessed with remarkable intelligence and wisdom, Abraham, even as a child, could not understand how his father could carve a statue with his own hands and then call it a god. The idea confused him and he worried about it day and night. Abraham would watch the priests lead the people in prayer in the temple, humbly beseeching the gods for help. He would, on many occasion, ask his father, in front of all the worshippers, "Did you not make these statues with your own hands? How then can you worship them and seek their help? Such statues cannot hear or understand anything. They cannot even hear each other."

> *'O my father! Why do you worship that which does not hear*
> *nor see, nor can it help you?*
> *O my father! I have been given a knowledge which you have not been*
> *given. O my father! Serve not the devil. Lo! the devil is a rebel to*
> *the All-Merciful. O my father! Lo! I fear lest a punishment from the All-*
> *Merciful overtake you so that you become a friend of the devil.'* (19:42-45)

Embarrassed by his son's questions, Abraham's father would scold him for talking so disrespectfully of the gods. But Abraham would not cease to criticise the gods, and, finally, his father said to him:

> *'Do you reject my gods, O Abraham? If you cease not, I shall surely stone you. Depart from me a long while.'* (19: 46)

Having failed to convince his father, Abraham turned to the people of his tribe, urging them to change the error of their ways.

> *'What are these images to which you are devoted?' They said: 'We found our fathers worshipping them.' He said, 'Verily you and your fathers were in plain error.' They said, 'Do you bring us the truth, or are you jesting?' He said, 'No but your Lord is the Lord of the Heavens and the Earth, Who created them; and I am of those who testify to that.'* (21: 52-56)

Seeing that gentle persuasion had no effect on his people, Abraham decided to resort to action. A great feast was to be held outside the town on a particular day. Abraham waited until everybody had left for the feast, then he hurried to the temple carrying a large axe. Making sure that no-one was nearby, he chopped off the head of one of the statues. Then, he proceeded to destroy all the statues in the temple except for the largest one on which he hung his axe.

When the feast was over, the people returned to the town. The first person to enter the temple was so horrified by the destruction of the statues, that he screamed out loud. When the people saw the state of their gods, their suspicion immediately fell on Abraham. They called Abraham and asked him,

> *'Are you the one that did this with our gods, O Abraham?' He said, 'Nay, this was done by their biggest one. Ask them if they can speak clearly!'*
> (21:62-63)

Abraham's words confused them, because they knew only too well that their gods could neither hear nor speak. Angered, they answered him,

> *'Well, you know that these speak not.' He said, 'Worship you then besides God things that can neither be of any good to you nor do you*

harm? Fie on you and on the things that you worship besides God! Have you no sense?' (21:65-67)

Thus Abraham silenced his people. But though they could not answer him, they knew that no-one else could have destroyed their gods and they decided to punish Abraham by burning him. A big fire was lit in the town square, and the people were summoned to come witness the death of the one who dared attack the gods. Abraham's hands and feet were tied up and he was then flung into the roaring fire.

Everyone waited as the fire burnt for many hours. When it finally died down, they saw that Abraham was sitting calmly in the middle quite unharmed by the fire. Even his clothes had no trace of ash, only the ropes tying his hands and feet had been burnt away. For God had said to the fire,

'O Fire, be coolness and peace for Abraham.' (21:69)

The story of Abraham's miraculous delivery from the fire reached the tyrant King who everyone feared, and Abraham was summoned to appear before him. When the King asked Abraham what his God was like, Abraham replied, "My God is He who gives life and takes it away." To this the arrogant King declared,

'I give life and cause death.' (2: 258)

For he could arrest any person in his kingdom and order him killed, or he could free any man who was condemned to death and thus give him life. Abraham then said,

'Lo ! God causes the sun to rise in the East. Can you cause it to rise from the West?' (2: 258)

The King had no reply to this and, angered, he dismissed Abraham. But by now, Abraham had realised that his people would never listen to the truth and he resolved to leave his homeland. Accompanied by his wife Sarah, and his nephew Lot, Abraham travelled to Syria, Palestine, and Egypt.

'I will leave home for the sake of my Lord.' (29:26)

For many years, Abraham and Sarah lived as exiles, and during all that time they had had no children. Sarah, having passed the age of childbirth, suggested to Abraham that he marry her maid and companion Hagar. Abraham and Hagar married and Hagar bore him a son who was called Ishmael. Many years later, God rewarded Sarah for her patience and faith by giving her a son of her own named Isaac, and tidings of a grandson named Jacob. God revealed that both Isaac and Jacob would become prophets.

But in the meantime, Abraham, Hagar and baby Ishmael set off on a journey. For days and nights they travelled, until they finally arrived at a barren valley in the desert of the Arabian peninsula. It was a desolate place with no vegetation and no water. There they stopped, and Abraham gave Hagar their remaining provisions of food and water. Surprised, Hagar asked, "Will you leave us here then?" Abraham made no reply. Once again, Hagar asked him if he would leave them in this place, and again Abraham made no response. She then realized that Abraham must be following a divine command and she asked him, "Did God command you to leave us here alone?" Abraham replied that such was the case, and Hagar declared, "We have God with us, no harm will come to us." And so, Hagar and Ishmael were left alone in this barren valley.

The heat was fierce and there was no shelter under which they could take refuge. Before long their provisions began to run low, and in desperation Hagar started looking for some water. Leaving Ishmael sitting on the ground, she ran to the top of a small hill called al-Ṣafā, hoping to see some sign of travellers who might be passing by and who would help them. There were none to be seen. Hagar went down to comfort Ishmael and then climbed up another hill, al-Marwa, in the hope of finding some help. Again she was disappointed. From al-Marwa she ran to al-Ṣafā, and then back to al-Marwa again. Seven times she climbed these hills and each time she saw nothing. Finally, when she returned to Ishmael, he was too weak to even cry. With great sorrow, Hagar bent down to pick him up, when lo and behold a spring gushed forth from under his feet! Hagar thanked God for saving them, and gave her son some water to drink.

It was not long before passing caravans noticed that birds had begun to gather in the barren valley where a spring of water now gushed. Soon travellers took to halting there and gradually people began to settle in this place. They called their little town Bakka, or Mecca. It was in this very town that, many years later, the prophet Muḥammad was born from the descendants of Ishmael and where he began preaching the message of Islam.

The years passed, and Ishmael grew into a handsome and intelligent young man. From time to time, Abraham would come to visit him and Hagar. One night, Abraham saw in a dream that he must sacrifice his son Ishmael. Now, although Abraham understood that this was a trial from God, he was deeply saddened as he loved Ishmael dearly. Nevertheless, Abraham did not question God's command and said to Ishmael,

> *'O my son! I saw in vision that I must offer you in sacrifice. What do you propose!'* (37:102)

Ishmael submitted to God's command without any hesitation and answered,

> *'O my father! Do what what you are commanded. God willing, you shall find me steadfast.'* (37:102)

Abraham took his son and went to a remote place to carry out God's command. However, just as he raised his hand to kill Ishmael, God ordered him to stop and to sacrifice a ram, which had miraculously appeared close to a nearby bush, instead. Abraham sacrificed the ram, then prostrated himself to God in gratitude for sparing his son. God had not wished to harm Abraham and Ishmael; He had wanted to try their obedience to Him and to make their obedience an example for generations to come. This event in the lives of Abraham and Ishmael is commemorated to this day by Muslims all over the world when sacrificing sheep on the ʿĪd al-Aḍḥā.

God revealed to Abraham that Mecca had always been a sacred place, where Adam himself had built a House for the worship of God. This House had been destroyed in the great Flood at the time of Noah. God now ordered Abraham and Ishmael to rebuild the Holy House, on the very same spot, and to make it a centre of pilgrimage. Gathering stones from the surrounding mountains, Abraham and Ishmael laid the foundations exactly as God commanded. While they worked, they invoked God's help and glorified Him.

'Accept this service from us: for You are the All-Hearing, the All-Knowing. Our Lord! make us submissive to you and of our progeny a people submissive to you. And show us our rites; and turn to us in Mercy; for You are the Forgiving, the Most Merciful. Our Lord! send them a messenger of their own, who shall reveal Your signs to them and instruct them in Scripture and Wisdom and sanctify them for You are the Exalted in Might, The Wise.' (2:127-129)

While Abraham and his son were working, angels descended from Heaven bearing a sacred stone. Abraham placed this stone, which is called al-Ḥajar al-Aswad or the Black Stone, in one of the corners of the Holy House or Kaʿba. When work on the Kaʿba was completed, God taught Abraham and Ishmael the rites that were to be performed there. All pilgrims to the Kaʿba must circle it seven times starting at the Black Stone, then they must walk between al-Ṣafā and al-Marwa seven times as Hagar had once done.

God then commanded Abraham to purify the Kaʿba for the pilgrims,

Behold! We gave the site of the Sacred House to Abraham. (Saying) 'Associate not anything (in worship) with Me, and sanctify My House for those who circle it, or stand up, or bow, or prostrate themselves (therein in prayer).' (22:26)

This done, Abraham wondered to himself if pilgrims would come to worship God in such an isolated place. But God, Who hears our innermost thoughts, said to him,

'And call men to the pilgrimage. They will come to you on foot and mounted on every kind of camel, lean on account of journeys through deep and distant mountain highways.' (22:27)

Abraham made the call and since then millions upon millions of pilgrims have come to visit the Kaʿba and to perform the pilgrimage. In fact, Muslims all over the world turn in the direction of the Kaʿba every day in their prayers or ṣalāt. And while Abraham, Ishmael and Hagar have passed away, their example lives on with us ever-new.

JOSEPH ﷺ & HIS DREAM

EARLIER WE saw how God blessed Sarah for her patience and faith by giving her a son, Isaac, and a grandson Jacob, both of whom were prophets. Jacob in turn had twelve sons. Of them all, the one he loved most was Joseph, a handsome boy of high intelligence and a kind nature. One night, as he slept, the young Joseph dreamt that the sun, the moon and eleven planets were prostrating themselves to him. When he woke up, he hurried to tell his father of his dream. On hearing Joseph's dream, Jacob understood that a great event lay in store for his young son. Jacob warned Joseph not to tell his brothers of his dream, lest they be envious and try to harm him, for Jacob knew that they were jealous of Joseph's favoured position.

'My little son, relate not your vision to your brothers lest they concoct a plot against you, for Satan is to man an avowed enemy.' (12:5)

One day, the ten elder brothers asked their father if they could take Joseph out hunting with them. Jacob was reluctant to agree, as he sensed that some danger might befall his favourite son. The brothers insisted however that no harm would come to Joseph, and, finally, Jacob relented. What Jacob did not know was that the brothers were planning, out of their jealousy, to rid themselves of Joseph. Shortly after they had left their father and were a distance from the town, they decided to carry out their terrible deed by throwing Joseph down a well and leaving him there to die. First, however, they stripped off his shirt and stained it with the blood of a sheep that they had slaughtered earlier. They then returned to Jacob, carrying the blood-stained shirt, weeping. "O father!" they cried, "that which you feared has come to pass! We left Joseph to look after our belongings while we ran races. No sooner had we turned our backs when a wolf, seeing that

Joseph was alone, attacked Joseph and ate him. Here is his shirt soaked with his blood." Jacob was sorely distressed, but in his heart he did not believe their story. He said,

> *'No, but you have plotted something. Patience is best for me and I will seek God's help concerning what you tell me.'* (12:18)

While his father grieved, Joseph lay at the bottom of the dark well, frightened and unable to get out. Soon, a caravan of travellers stopped to draw water. When they lowered a bucket into the well, Joseph held on to it and was pulled to the top. Imagine the surprise of the travellers when they saw a handsome boy emerging from the well! They decided to take him with them to Egypt in the hope of selling him there for a good price.

When the caravan arrived in Egypt, Joseph was sold to a nobleman who took him into his service. Quickly the nobleman and his wife became fond of Joseph, for the young boy was not only handsome but also good-natured and intelligent.

The years passed and Joseph grew into a young man of stunning beauty and charm. This, however, proved to be a source of trouble for him, for his master's wife fell in love with him and tried to tempt him. When Joseph rejected her advances, the outraged wife unjustly accused him of misbehaving towards her and Joseph was thrown into prison.

Joseph did not enter prison as a common criminal, for he was innocent and had a clear conscience. He was resigned to waiting for God's justice and regarded his imprisonment as a blessing which kept him from the temptation with which he had been tested at his master's house. And yet, there was another reason for Joseph being in prison, for it was while he was there that Joseph received God's call to be a prophet, thus following in the footsteps of his father Jacob, his grandfather Isaac, and his great-grandfather Abraham. And so, Joseph began his mission while in prison and would preach to his fellow prisoners. He would urge the criminals to abandon their wicked ways and he would console those wrongly imprisoned and bid them endure their suffering patiently.

> *'I have I assure you abandoned the ways of a people that believe not in God and that even deny the Hereafter. And I follow the ways of my fathers, Abraham, Isaac and Jacob; and never could we attribute any partners whatever to God. That is a result of the grace of God to us and to mankind; yet most men are not grateful.' (12:37-38)*

There was another gift with which Joseph was blessed, the gift of interpreting dreams. One day, two of his companions in prison came to Joseph and asked him to interpret their dreams. Before their imprisonment both men had worked at the palace of the King of Egypt. Now, the first had dreamt that he was standing on a high place, carrying bread on his head and that birds were eating the bread. The second man had dreamt that he was offering wine to the King. Joseph listened carefully to what his two companions related and thought for a while. Then, he told the first man that he was going to be crucified. Joseph told the second man that he would return to the palace and pour out wine for his King to drink. Joseph then asked the man he knew would be released, to remind the King that he was still in prison, and to tell him that he had been wronged and was awaiting his release.

Not long afterwards, Joseph's predictions came true. The first man was condemned to death and the second was released and returned to the palace. The second man, however, forgot to remind the King about Joseph, and so Joseph remained in prison for several more years.

One night, the King had a very strange dream which he failed to understand. He called for all of the priests of the land to come to him in order to interpret his dream. The King then told them how in a dream he had seen seven fat cows being eaten by seven lean cows, and seven green ears of corn followed by seven dry ears. None of the priests could interpret the dream. It was only then that the cup-bearer remembered Joseph. He announced to the King that Joseph had the power to interpret dreams. The King immediately sent one of his men to ask Joseph about the meaning of his dream.

Joseph replied that Egypt will witness seven years of prosperity followed by seven years of hardship. He advised the King to store the surplus grain of the first seven years in order to be able to feed his people during the seven lean years. The King was satisfied with this interpretation of his dream and, realizing that Joseph was gifted with great knowledge, sent for Joseph to be brought to him. To the King's amazement, Joseph refused to leave the prison until the King had recognized his innocence. When Joseph's case was looked into, it became clear that Joseph indeed was innocent of the accusations made against him. Impressed by his honesty, the King said,

'Bring him to me; I will take him to serve me alone.' (12:54)

When Joseph was told of the King's wishes, he replied,

'Set me over the store-houses of the land: I will indeed guard them, as one that knows their importance.' (12:55)

The King consented to his request, and Joseph devoted himself faithfully to his task. During the seven years of prosperity, he ordered that the surplus grain be saved. But after these seven years came seven years of hardship, and famine spread everywhere in Egypt and the surrounding countries.

Joseph began to distribute what had been saved, giving each person what he needed. He was a very wise man, for God had endowed him with great knowledge. Word of Joseph's wisdom spread and before long tribes in neighbouring lands were also coming to him for food.

Among those who came to Egypt were Joseph's elder brothers. As was the case everywhere else, food had become scarce in their land and they had come to seek provisions from the King of Egypt's minister. Little did they know that the minister was their brother Joseph who they presumed dead. When Joseph's brothers entered the palace, Joseph immediately recognized them. They, not surprisingly, did not recognize him, for it never occurred to them that the young boy who they had thrown down a well, could not only survived, but had also risen to such high rank.

Joseph asked about their situation and about the number of people in their family in order to give them the exact amount of grain that they needed. They told him that they had a younger brother who had been left at home with their father. So Joseph asked them to bring him when they returned for provisions the following year. Secretly, he longed very much to see his younger brother Benjamin; so he threatened them that if they failed to bring him, he would not give them any food.

The brothers went home with enough provisions for one year. When the time came for them to return to Egypt in order to obtain grain for the following year, they asked their father for permission to take their younger brother with them. Jacob feared for his son, remembering what had happened to Joseph.

> *'Shall I entrust him to you as I had previously entrusted his brother?'*
> (12:64)

Their urgent need for food, however, made Jacob accept to send his youngest son with his brothers. But he made them promise to take good care of him and bring him back safely.

The caravan carrying Jacob's sons arrived in Egypt and proceeded to the palace. When the brothers entered, Joseph took Benjamin aside and confided to him that he was Joseph. He asked him not to reveal this to their other brothers. Joseph had decided to keep Benjamin with him in Egypt and, to this end, he had thought up a plan to prevent him from leaving with the others. Joseph ordered that provisions be supplied for the caravan. Then, as the brothers were preparing to depart, it was announced that the King's silver cup, with which the grain was measured, was missing. Joseph ordered that the caravan be searched. To the brothers protestations that they had not stolen anything, Joseph responded,

> *'What then shall be the penalty of this, if you are proved to have lied?'*
>
> (12:74)

The brothers answered,

> *'The penalty should be that he in whose saddle-bag it is found, should have the law applied to him.'* (12:75)

It was Abraham's law that the victim of a theft was entitled to take the thief as a slave in compensation for the crime committed against him. When the caravans were searched, the cup was found in Benjamin's bag and consequently Joseph had the right to keep his brother.

The brothers returned to their father and told him that their younger brother had stolen the cup, and that the minister had kept him with him as punishment. The brothers swore to their father that this was the truth, and they even made the people of the caravan bear witness. Jacob, however, did not believe them and thought that they had plotted to get rid of their youngest brother just as they had plotted against Joseph; he wept with grief until he went blind. He then ordered them to return to Egypt to try and find news of their brother as well as of Joseph.

> *'O my sons! go and enquire about Joseph and his brother, and never give up hope of God's soothing Mercy; truly no one despairs of God's soothing Mercy, except those who have no faith.'* (12:87)

So Jacob's sons returned to Egypt and pleaded with Joseph to release their younger brother, since their father was an old man who deeply grieved for his son. To their pleadings, Joseph replied,

> *'Do you know how you dealt with Joseph and his brother, not knowing what you were doing?'* (12:89)

At once the brothers realized that they were in the presence of Joseph. At first, they feared that he might want to punish them, but he treated them kindly. Then Joseph took his shirt off and gave it to his brothers, telling them to return with it to their father and to cast it upon his face. This, he said, would restore his sight. He then requested them to bring the whole family to Egypt.

Greatly relieved and grateful, the brothers went home. As they approached their land and were only a few days journey from home, Jacob sensed that they were near because he could smell the scent of Joseph's shirt. He told his family,

'I do indeed scent Joseph; and I am not making it up.' (12:94)

The people around Jacob thought that he had lost his mind. Shortly afterwards, however, the caravan arrived bringing Joseph's shirt. The brothers laid it on their father's face as Joseph had instructed, and Jacob's sight was restored.

'Did I not say to you, "I know from God that which you know not?"'
They said, 'O our father! Ask for us forgiveness for our sins, for we were
truly at fault.' He said, 'I will ask my Lord for forgiveness for you, for He
is indeed Forgiving, Most Merciful.' (12:96-98)

The whole of Joseph's family then departed for Egypt. On arriving there, they were able to see the rank to which Joseph had risen, and they all prostrated themselves before him in awe. In this way, the dream that Joseph had had as a boy, of the sun, the moon and eleven stars prostrating themselves before him, was realised. Overwhelmed with gratitude to God for delivering him from prison, for re-uniting him with his father and for guiding his brothers back to the right path, Joseph prostrated himself before God, saying,

'O my Lord! You have indeed bestowed on me power, and taught me the
interpretation of dreams. O You creator of the heavens and the earth! You
are my Protector in this world and in the Hereafter. Take You my soul at
death as one submitting to Your Will, and unite me with the righteous.'

(12:101)

MOSES ﷺ & THE PHARAOH

Jacob and his sons settled in Egypt at the invitation of Joseph whose power in the land was second only to that of the King. When Jacob sensed that his death was near, he summoned his sons and questioned them about their faith.

> *'What will you worship after me?' They said, 'We shall worship your God, the God of your fathers, Abraham, Ishmael and Isaac, One God, and to Him we have surrendered.'* (2:133)

Now, Jacob was also known as Israel and his sons and descendants were called the Children of Israel or the Israelites. After his death, Jacob's sons remained in Egypt and enjoyed the protection of their brother Joseph. But the time came when Joseph also passed away. The Children of Israel, however, grew in number and strength and soon became a force to be reckoned with in Egypt.

Then, to the throne of Egypt, came a king who took the name of Pharaoh. Pharaoh greatly feared the Children of Israel, for it had been foretold that one of them would cause the downfall of his kingdom. Now, Pharoah was particularly cruel and unjust, and one of the first things he did when he came to the throne was to order that all the baby boys of the Children of Israel be killed. It was during this terrible time that a very pious woman of the Children of Israel gave birth to a son who she called Moses. Fearing that her child may be killed, Moses' mother kept him hidden. But one night, while she was feeding him, God ordered Moses' mother to place him in a basket and set the basket afloat on the river Nile.

> *'Put him into the basket, and throw it into the river, then the river shall*

throw it onto the bank, and there an enemy to Me and an enemy to him shall take him.' (20:39)

Afraid but obedient, Moses' mother took the small baby to the river and placed him in a basket which she left right by the water's edge. She looked on with a heavy heart as the current gently carried the basket away. And yet, she had no reason to fear, for God protected the baby for whom He had planned a great future.

While the basket floated gently downstream, baby Moses slept peacefully. Eventually, the basket came to rest on a bank overlooked by Pharaoh's palace. Now, it came to pass that Pharoah's wife was taking a walk that morning in the palace gardens when she noticed the basket. She sent one of her ladies-in-waiting to see what it contained. To her surprise and delight, the lady-in-waiting returned carrying a beautiful baby fast asleep. Although Pharaoh was cruel and unjust, his wife was humble and good. She took the baby in her arms and went to ask her husband whether they could keep him. At first Pharaoh would not agree. But such was the pleading of his wife, that eventually Pharaoh accepted that the baby be brought up at the palace.

Before long the baby awoke and began to cry from hunger. Pharaoh's wife ordered the child to be taken to a woman to nurse him, but the baby refused to suckle. So he was sent to another nurse, and then another, but still he would not feed. Pharaoh's wife became seriously worried.

At Moses' home, his mother was unable to rest. Her anxiety grew and grew until she could no longer bear not knowing what had happened to her son. Finally, she asked her daughter to try and find some news. The girl walked to the city and, as she passed Pharaoh's palace, she overheard the servants talking about a small baby discovered on the water's edge, and of the concern of Pharaoh's wife for the life of the baby, as it refused to feed.

From the description, the girl immediately realised that they must be talking about her brother Moses. She quickly went up to them and told them that she knew of someone who could feed the baby, and if Pharaoh's wife agreed, she would bring the woman at once. Pharaoh's wife, who was by now desperate, promised the woman anything if the baby would accept her. Moses' sister ran home and, with her mother, hurried back to the palace. As soon as Moses' mother took him in her arms, he nursed happily and then fell into a contented sleep. Pharaoh's wife was delighted that the baby's life was no longer in danger, and agreed that this woman should become the infant's nursemaid.

> *And we restored you to your mother that her eyes might be cooled from weeping and that she might not sorrow.* (20:40)

Moses' mother was overjoyed and thanked God from the depths of her heart for the return of her child, who would now be under the protection and care of Pharaoh, the very same person who had ordered that all the Children of Israel's baby boys be killed. Never could she have imagined that her child would be brought up at the court and would study under the greatest scholars of the land. Yet, that was all part of God's plan for Moses.

One day, Moses, now a young man, was walking through the city when he came upon two men fighting. One was a follower of Pharaoh, the other was one of the Children of Israel. Moses went to help the weaker of the two, which happened to be the Israelite, and pushed the follower of Pharaoh with his hand. The man fell to the ground and was killed, such was the strength of Moses. Moses returned to the palace deeply regretting what had taken place.

The next day he walked through the city cautiously listening for any news of the previous day's events. Unexpectedly, he came across the same man that he had saved the previous day fighting with another man. Moses walked up to him and chastised him for his behaviour. The man retorted,

> *'O Moses! will you kill me as you killed a person yesterday?'* (28:19)

Moses feared that Pharaoh would hear of the accident and think instead that Moses had killed one of Pharaoh's followers on purpose. And Moses was right to fear, for it was not long before he was informed that Pharaoh had heard of the death of his follower and that Pharaoh's ministers were plotting against Moses. Moses knew that he must flee Egypt at once.

> *'My Lord! Deliver me from the wrongdoing folk.'* (28:21)

Moses left Egypt secretly on foot. He walked day and night through the desert, eating berries and grass until he reached the edge of the desert. There he came upon a group of shepherds with their flocks at a well. The shepherds were arguing over who should water his sheep first. Moses was able to quench his thirst at the well, then he sat down to rest in the shade of a tree. As he sat, he saw two girls with their sheep some distance away from the crowds. He went over to them and asked them why they had not joined the other shepherds. They replied that they were forced to wait until the other shepherds had finished, for their father was very old and they had to take care of all the sheep. Upon hearing this, Moses immediately took their flock and drove it through the crowd to the water. When the sheep had been watered the girls thanked him and Moses returned to rest under the tree.

Not long after, one of the two girls returned and asked Moses to come and meet their father as he wanted to thank him for helping his daughters. The old man asked Moses where he had come from, and Moses told him that he had fled from Egypt to escape the wrath of Pharaoh. The old man said to Moses, "You are now out of Pharaoh's realm. Stay here and live in peace." He asked Moses to stay as his guest.

After some time, the old man said,

> *'I have intended to wed one of my daughters to you, on condition that you serve me for eight years.'* (28:27)

Moses would then be free to stay or to leave. Moses agreed to this offer.

Eight years went by and Moses was now free to leave. He decided that he should return to Egypt. Although he could not explain his decision, he knew it was God's will. And so Moses took his wife and family and headed for Egypt.

One cold, dark night, while crossing the desert, Moses lost his way. He tried to build a fire to help him see where he was, but the wind and rain were so strong that the fire kept going out. Looking around him, Moses noticed a fire in the distance, on the side of a mountain. He asked his family to wait for him while he went to collect an ember from that fire.

> *'Stay here! I see in the distance a fire. Perhaps I shall bring you something of it or a brand from the fire that you may warm yourselves.'* (28:29)

Moses was in the valley and he started climbing towards the fire he could see on the side of the mountain. As he approached the fire, Moses noticed that as bright as the flame was, the bush that it burnt from remained green. At that moment God spoke to Moses,

> *'O Moses! I, even I, am your Lord. So take off your shoes, for lo! you are in the holy valley of Tuwa. I have chosen you, so hearken to that which is inspired. Lo! I, even, I, am God. There is no God save Me. So serve Me and establish worship for My remembrance. Lo! The hour is surely coming. But I will to keep it hidden, that every soul may be rewarded for that which it strived after.'* (20:11-16)

The earth shook at these words and Moses stood in awe, trembling from fear. Overcoming his fear, he took off his sandals and prostrated himself in humility and respect. God then spoke again,

> *'And what is that in your right hand, O Moses?'* (20:17)

Moses answered God saying,

> *'This is my staff, on it I lean, and with it I beat down branches for my sheep, and for it I find other uses.'* (20:18)

God said,

> *'Cast it down, O Moses!'* (20:19)

Moses cast it down, and it turned into a snake gliding on the ground. Moses shrank back in fear; but God said to him,

> *'Grasp it and fear not. We shall return it to its former state.'* (20:21)

As soon as Moses grasped the snake it turned back into a staff. God then ordered Moses to put his hand inside his shirt and draw it out again. Moses did as he was ordered, and his hand came out luminous, shining bright. God then told Moses to place his hand on his heart, and when Moses did this he felt great peace and serenity. God had shown Moses these two miracles as proof of His Power, and they marked the beginning of Moses's mission. For God had chosen Moses as His messenger to Pharaoh and his people, calling them to worship the One God.

Moses, remembering that he had killed one of Pharaoh's followers, was afraid to return Egypt alone, and asked God if he may take his brother Aaron with him.

> *'And give me an aide from my family, Aaron my brother, that I may gain strength through him and that he may share my task, that we may celebrate Your praise without stint and remember You without stint, for we are ever in Your Sight.'* (20:29-35)

God consented to his request, and reassured Moses, saying,

> *'Fear not, for I am with you; I hear and see (everything).'* (20:46)

Thus, Moses returned to his family who had been waiting for him in the valley. He recounted to them his meeting with God and together they set off anew for Egypt.

Moses finally arrived in Egypt and went straight to Pharaoh's palace to convey to him the message from God. At first, Pharaoh was surprised to see that Moses had dared return to Egypt. But his surprise gave way to fury when he heard what Moses had to say. Moses told Pharaoh that he must give up worshipping other than the One God, and that he must allow the Children of Israel to practice their religion freely, for Pharaoh had placed very harsh and strict rules upon them. Pharaoh's answer was,

> *'If you choose a god other than me, I shall surely imprison you.'* (26:29)

Moses said to Pharaoh,

> *'And what if I bring you proof of my message?'* (26:30)

Pharaoh said, "Show us your proof."

> *Then he (Moses) flung down his staff and it was clearly a serpent, and he drew forth his hand, and lo! it was white to the beholders.* (26: 29-33)

These were the two miracles that God had given Moses as a support for his mission. But Pharaoh was stubborn and accused Moses of magic. He ordered Moses to return at a later time, when a contest would be held between Moses and the best magicians in the land.

> *He said, 'Have you come to drive us out of our land by your magic, O Moses? But we surely can produce magic to match yours; so appoint a*

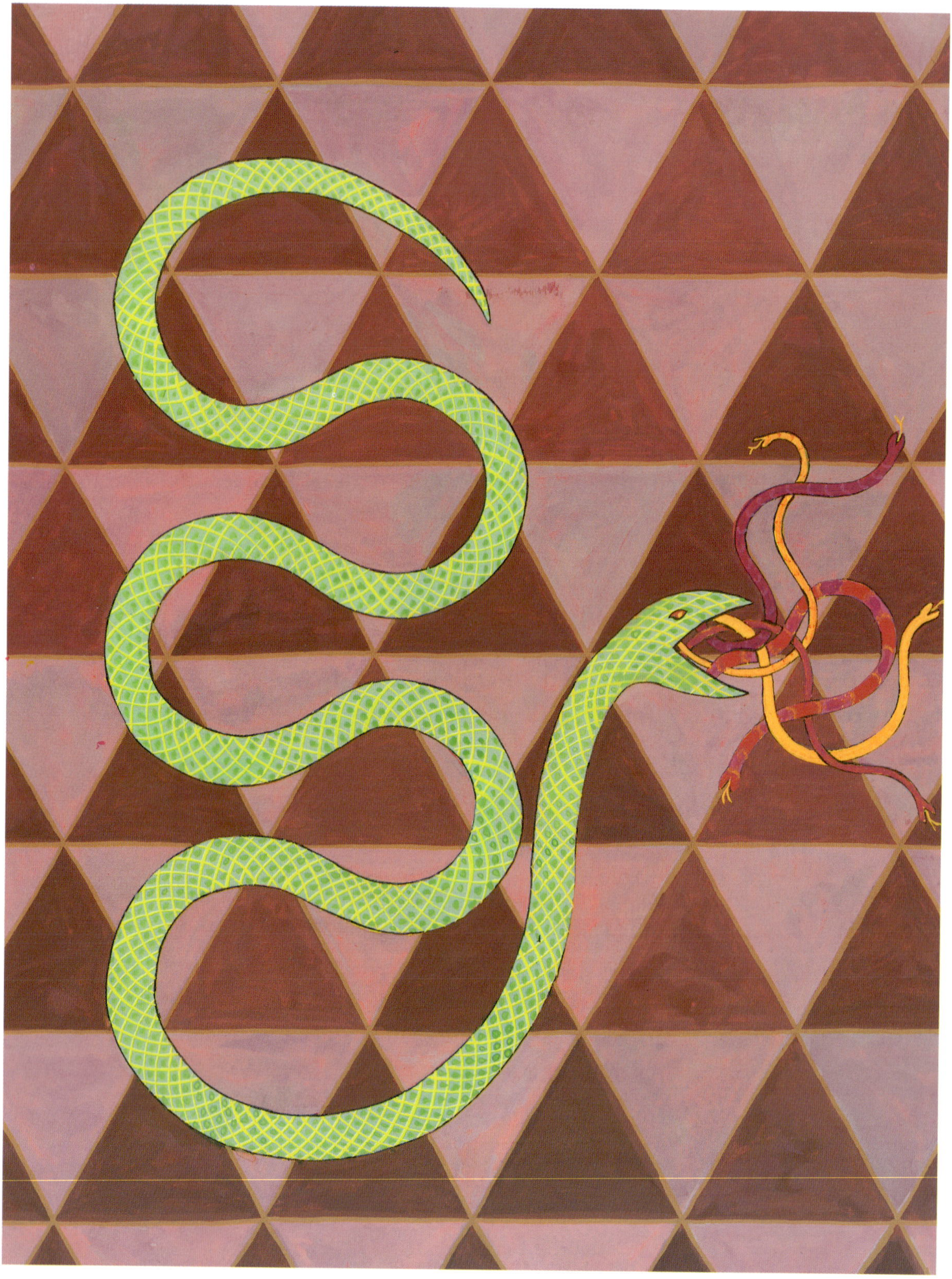

> *fixed date between us and you, which neither we nor you shall fail to keep, at a place convenient (to us both).'* (20:57-58)

The day agreed upon was called the Day of the Feast, and Pharaoh had gathered all the best magicians of the land to compete with Moses. During the course of the morning, people began assembling in a large square outside the town. By the time that Pharaoh arrived accompanied by the highest magicians, a huge crowd had already gathered. Everyone was curious to see how Moses, with his brother by his side, would confront Pharaoh.

It was decided that the magicians should start the contest. The magicians began by throwing ropes on the ground and, using their magic, they made the ropes appear to move like snakes. On seeing this, Moses was frightened. But God inspired him to cast down his staff which became a large snake that swallowed up all of the magicians' ropes.

> *Lo! that which they have made is but a wizard's doing, and a wizard shall not be successful, to whatever point (of skill) he may attain.* (20:69)

The magicians knew all about magic and, when they saw what Moses had done, they understood immediately that it was not magic but that Moses must have the help of God. When they told this to Pharaoh, he was furious and threatened to have his magicians crucified. The magicians, however, were not shaken by his threats and declared their belief in the God of Moses and in Moses as a prophet.

Pharaoh's ministers insisted that he punish Moses as well as the magicians. For Pharaoh must never tolerate such a threat to his power and position.

> *The chiefs of Pharaoh's people said, '(O King) you suffer Moses and his people to make mischief in the land, and to reject you and your gods?' He said, 'We will slay their sons, and spare their women, for lo! we are in power over them.'* (7:127)

Moses encouraged those who believed in him to be patient and to remain firm in their faith in the hope that Pharaoh and his people may one day believe in God.

And Moses said to his people, 'Seek help in God and endure. Lo! the earth is God's. He gives it for an inheritance to whom He will. And lo! the righteous will have a good end.' (7:128)

Moses remained in Egypt for many years reminding its people of the grace and mercy of God and warning them of the punishment they would receive if they persisted in their ways. However, the people of Egypt refused to believe the message that Moses brought, for they feared Pharaoh more than they feared God.

Then, God sent one punishment after another to Pharaoh and his people. He made the river Nile flood and caused its waters to cover the entire land for a long period. He followed this by a plague of locusts which ate all of the crops; then by a plague of lice; then by a plague of frogs that multiplied at a tremendous rate which horrified people. Finally, the water of the Nile turned into blood. Each time the people of Egypt suffered one of these punishments they went to Moses and implored him to ask his God to rid them of their trial. And they promised that they would worship God, and allow the Children of Israel to leave Egypt with Moses.

And when the terror fell on them, they cried, 'O Moses! on our behalf call on your Lord in virtue of His promise to you. If you remove the terror from us, we surely will trust you and will let the Children of Israel go with you.' (7:128)

However, each time God relieved the people from their ordeal, they failed to honour their promises and returned to their old ways and continued to persecute the Children of Israel. Moses finally realized that Pharaoh and the people of Egypt would never change nor would they ever accept his message. He decided to leave Egypt and to take with him those of the Children of Israel who believed in his message. He asked them to prepare themselves secretly, fearing the punishment of Pharaoh.

When Moses and his followers were all ready, they quickly left the city under cover of darkness. But soon Pharaoh learnt of their escape. Enraged, he gathered up his army and set off in pursuit. Before long, Pharaoh's army had Moses and his followers in sight. The Children of Israel were terrified when they saw the soldiers advancing upon them and said to Moses,

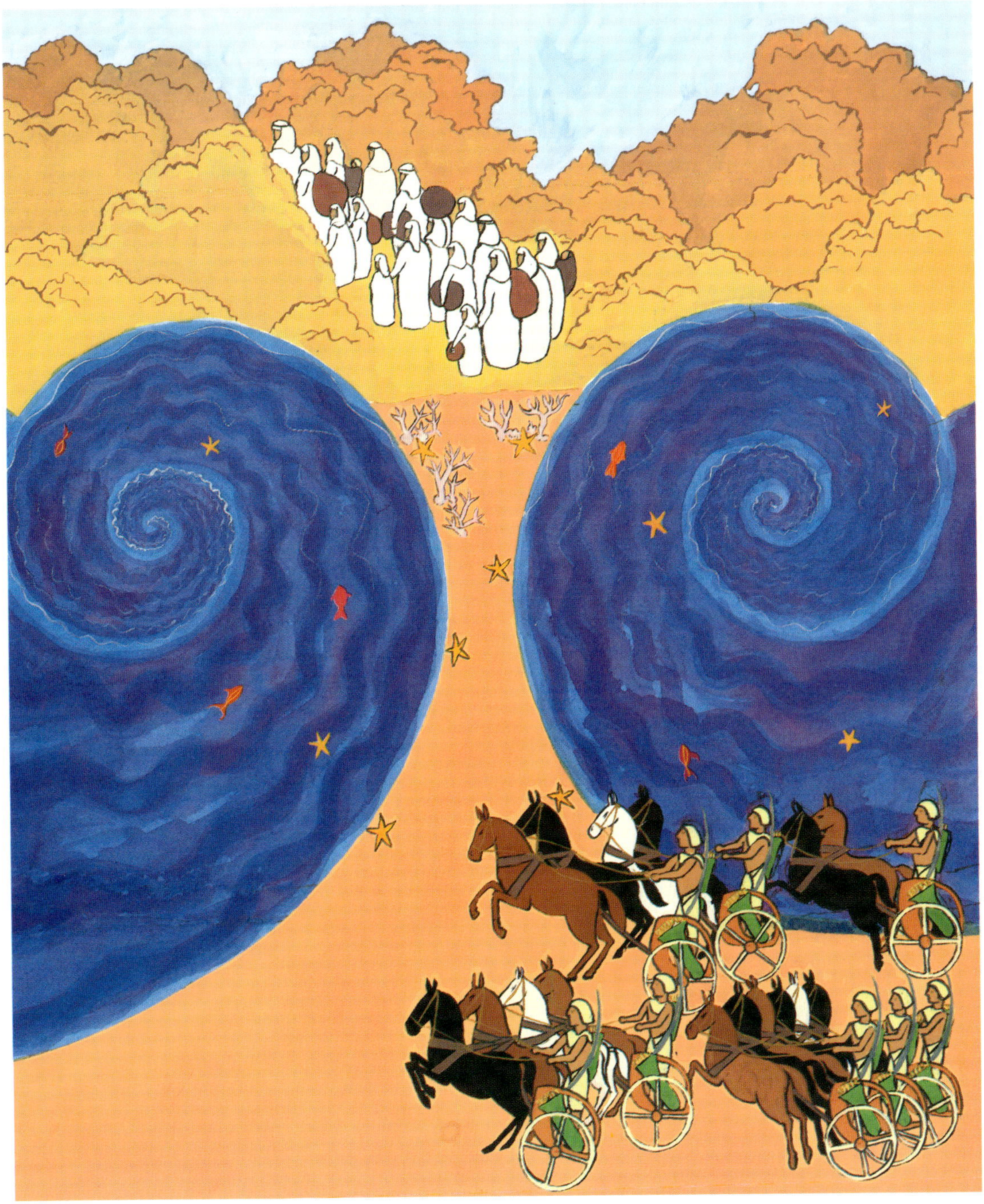

> *'We are indeed caught.' He said, 'No, my Lord is with me. He will guide me.'* (26:61-62)

But there was nowhere to escape, for the Red Sea lay in front of Moses and his followers and the enemy behind. As Pharaoh and his troops drew nearer, hemming them in, God inspired Moses to strike the sea with his staff. Moses struck the sea, and the sea divided itself into two, leaving a dry path in front of Moses and his followers. Overjoyed, they hurried across the path that God had made for them. And no sooner had they crossed safely, when Pharaoh arrived at the other side. Unmoved by the marvellous miracle he was witnessing, Pharaoh ordered his troops to follow Moses between the two great walls of water. But they were only half way across, when God made the sea close up again. In horror, Pharaoh and his men saw the walls of water rejoining, while they were still on the path. And thus they were all drowned.

> *And we saved Moses and all who were with him; but We drowned the others.* (26:65-66)

Moses guided his people through the desert after their escape from Pharaoh. It was during this journey that God gave Moses the Torah, the Holy Book of the Children of Israel. The Torah contains all the laws which allow the Children of Israel to live their lives in accordance with God's Will.

❖

DAVID ﷷ AND SOLOMON ﷷ

AFTER THE DEATH of Moses, the Children of Israel put all the things they considered sacred into a special chest called the Ark of the Covenant. Among what was included in the Ark of the Covenant were the clay tablets on which their sacred book, the Torah, was written as well as the staff of Moses which God had transformed twice into a snake. Whenever the Children of Israel went into battle, they would send the Ark with the vanguard. This reassured them greatly and gave them certainty of victory.

Gradually, however, the Children of Israel strayed from the path which Moses had shown them. As a punishment for their disobedience, God sent them an enemy who drove them out of their land, stole the Ark, and sowed the seeds of division among them. For years, the Children of Israel lived in exile, until God forgave them and sent them a prophet called Samuel to guide them. The prophethood of Samuel raised the hopes of the Children of Israel, and they asked him to choose for them a king who would unite them, and help them fight against their enemy. Samuel chose a man called Saul, or Ṭālūt, to be their king.

Their prophet said to them, 'God has appointed Ṭālūt as a king over you.'
(2:247)

Saul decided to lead the Children of Israel into battle to regain the Ark of the Covenant. But when the Children of Israel arrived at the battleground, they were taken aback by the size of their enemy's army. At the head of that army was Goliath, a man whose strength, bravery and skill in battle were renowned throughout the land.

When the moment came for the two armies to confront each other,

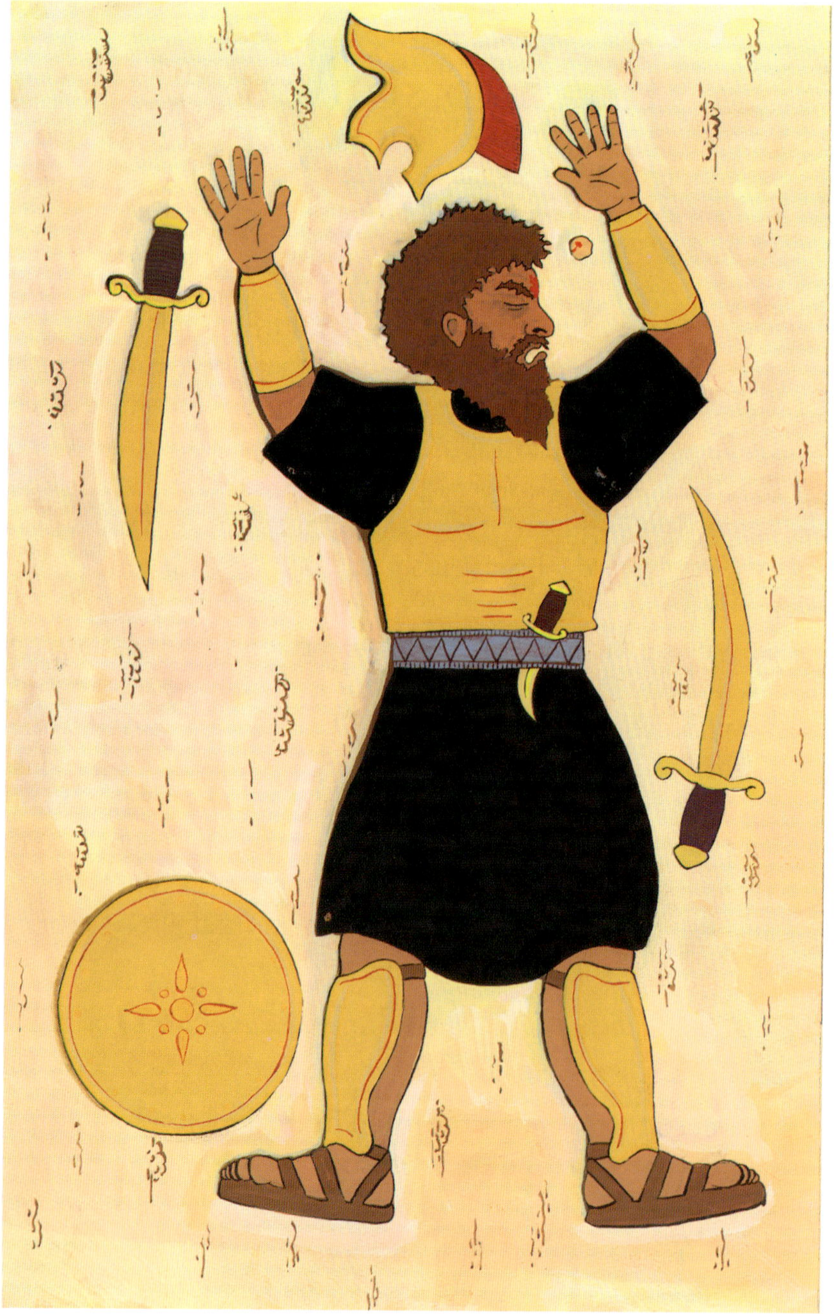

Goliath appeared brandishing his sword and challenging any of the Children of Israel to come forth and meet him in combat. Now, among the army of Saul was a young shepherd called David. David possessed no arms except for a slingshot and a few stones. But despite his youth and lack of arms, David stepped forward and accepted the challenge. Everyone was surprised at his great courage, and Goliath made fun of his reckless bravery. How dare David confront the strongest hero who is feared by everyone in the country?

Unmoved by Goliath's imposing stature and mocking comments, David took up his position in front of Goliath, and quickly fired a shot at him with his sling. The stone hit Goliath hard on the forehead and he fell to the ground dead. On seeing that their leader had been killed by a young man, Goliath's army ran away and were pursued by Saul's men.

> *And David slew Goliath; and God gave him power and wisdom and taught him whatever else He willed. And did not God check one set of people by means of another, the earth would indeed be full of mischief, but God is full of bounty to all the worlds.* (2:251)

Thus the Children of Israel had gained victory solely through David's courage. In order to reward him, Saul made David his co-regent and gave him his daughter in marriage.

At the death of Saul, David became the king of the Children of Israel. But David was not only a king, for God had chosen David as a prophet, and had revealed to him a heavenly book called the Book of Psalms.

> *And to David We gave the Psalms.* (4:163)

The Psalms were prayers to God, and David loved to chant them out loud; his voice was considered to be the most beautiful on earth. Occasionally, David would go out into the wilderness to chant; then the birds in the sky would stop flying, the wind would stop blowing, the wild animals would gather around him, and the mountains, the valleys, and the trees would echo his prayers.

> *It was We that made the hills declare, in unison with him, Our Praises, at eventide and at break of day; and the birds gathered in assemblies, all with him did turn to God.* (38:18-19)

There was one other gift that God had bestowed upon David. This gift was the ability to shape iron with his bare hands. God rendered iron soft in the hands of David, and the skill with which he worked had never been seen before. With iron David made armour, and many victories were won because of the protection which the armour gave the Children of Israel.

> *We bestowed grace on David from Us, 'O you mountains sing you back the praises of God with him and you birds also.' And We made the iron soft for him.* (34:10)

And so, David lived life worshipping God and organizing the affairs of his people with justice, wisdom and mercy. He was a pious and just ruler, and thus earned rewards both in this life and in the Hereafter.

When David died, his son Solomon inherited his position as prophet and king of the Children of Israel. God bestowed many favours upon Solomon, just like He had done with his father before him. And, as can be seen from this story, Solomon had already shown signs of these great gifts when still a child. Solomon was once in the company of his father, when two men came to ask David to judge between them. The first of the two said that he owned a vineyard of which he took great care the whole year through. But one day when he was absent, the other man's sheep had strayed into the vineyard and devoured its grapes. He asked to be compensated for this damage. Upon hearing the man's complaint, Solomon suggested that the owner of the sheep take the other man's vineyard to repair and cultivate until the vines returned to their former state, whereupon he should return it to its owner. Meanwhile, the owner of the vineyard would care for the sheep and benefit from their wool and milk until his land was returned to him, at which time he would return the sheep to their owner. This sound judgement showed that Solomon already possessed much wisdom at an early age. Wisdom, in fact, would always be associated with Solomon, who later in life came to be known as Solomon the Wise.

When Solomon became king, he addressed the following prayer to God,

> *'O my Lord! Forgive me, and grant me a Kingdom which You will grant no-one after me, for You are the Grantor of Bounties without measure.'*
>
> (38:35)

God accepted Solomon's prayer and granted him a kingdom which had been granted to no-one before him. God also made the wind subservient to Solomon blowing wherever he wished; He brought the *jinn* under Solomon's command, they obeyed his orders and accomplished for him what human beings could not do. Moreover, God taught Solomon the languages of the birds and the animals.

Once, as Solomon was marching at the head of his army, he entered a valley inhabited by hoards of ants. On seeing the army, one of the ants called to the others,

'O ants! enter your dwellings lest Solomon and his armies crush you,
without knowing.' (27:18)

Solomon understood what the ant had said and smiled to himself. Solomon was grateful to God for the many blessings He had granted him, and every incident in his life, no matter how small, gave him opportunity to thank his Lord.

'O my Lord! help me to thank you for Your favours, which You have
bestowed on me and on my parents, and to act righteously to please you
and admit me, by Your Grace, to the ranks of Your Righteous Servants.'
                                                                    (28:19)

As we have seen, Solomon was famous for his great wisdom which had first shown itself when he was but a child. As a king, Solomon used his wisdom to judge between people. There is a famous story always given as an example of Solomon's wisdom. One day, two women were having a dispute over a child, each claiming to be the infant's mother. So they went to ask Solomon to judge who the child belonged to. Solomon said that he could not tell who the real mother was, and told the women that the best solution would be to cut the child into two equal parts so that each woman could have her share. On hearing this the real mother cried out, "Take him, I do not want my part!" From this outburst, Solomon knew that this woman was the true mother, because she preferred to give up her child rather than have him harmed, and so he gave the infant to her.

The power that God had given Solomon over the *jinn* and the other creatures, enabled him to use them in his army. Often the *jinn* would make

52

his army appear greater in size than it really was, and often the birds would fly in flocks overhead to scout for him and to shade his troops from the heat of the sun.

One day, when Solomon was inspecting his troops, he found that one of the birds, the hoopoe, was not in its usual place. This angered him, and he threatened to punish him severely.

> *And he surveyed the birds; and he said, 'Why is it that I do not see the Hoopoe? or is he among the absentees? I will certainly punish him with a severe penalty, or execute him, unless he bring me a clear reason for absence.' (27:20-21)*

Shortly afterwards, the hoopoe returned in a great hurry and stood before Solomon saying,

> *'I have been to a territory which you have not been to, and I have come to you from Sheba with true tidings.' (27:22)*

The hoopoe had important news for his master. He had discovered a kingdom called the Kingdom of Sheba. This kingdom was ruled by a powerful woman, and she and her people worshipped the sun instead of God. Solomon listened carefully, with great interest, then said firmly,

> *'Soon shall we see whether you have told the truth or lied!' (27:27)*

Solomon wrote a letter to the Queen of Sheba urging her to follow his religion and to worship God. He then gave the letter to the hoopoe instructing him to take it to the Queen. He told him to throw the letter in front of her, and then hide and observe her reaction. The hoopoe was then to return to Solomon and inform him of what had taken place.

Off flew the hoopoe to the palace of Sheba and dropped the letter at the feet of the Queen, then hid as he had been told. The Queen opened the letter and started reading it with great interest. When she had finished, she called her ministers and the elders of her people to come before her in order to discuss the contents of the letter.

> *'O chiefs! here is delivered to me a letter worthy of respect.' (27:29)*

They all waited to hear the contents of the letter. The Queen read,

'It is from Solomon, and is as follows, "In the name of God, Most Gracious, Most Merciful! Be you not arrogant against me, but come to me in submission to the true Religion"' (27:30-31)

Everybody kept quiet waiting for the Queen's answer. But she told them that she wanted to take council with them and that she would not accomplish anything without their advice.

'O chiefs! Advise me in this my affair; no affair have I decided except in your presence.' (27:32)

54

Both the ministers and the elders replied that they were ready to fight if she wished, since they were strong enough and had the necessary weapons. They left it up to her to decide what to do. The Queen, however, did not wish to engage in war since she did not know how strong Solomon and his army were, and she did not want to destroy her kingdom through ignorance.

So she decided to reply to Solomon's letter by sending him gifts in order to win his friendship. The Queen chose some of her men and sent them to Solomon with valuable presents. When they arrived at the kingdom of Solomon, they were completely taken aback by the grandeur that God had bestowed upon Solomon. They saw things in his kingdom that they had never seen or heard of before. The men offered the presents to Solomon who looked at them with disdain and said,

> *'Will you give me more wealth? But that which God has given me is better than that which He has given you! No it is you who rejoice in your gift!'*
>
> (27:36)

Solomon did not accept the Queen of Sheba's presents, and told the envoys to inform the Queen that she had to choose between two things: she can either accept his religion or he would send his army, in all its strength, to drive her and her people out of their land. The envoys hurried back to their country to inform the Queen of all that had happened. She listened to their story and realized that Solomon was different from all the other kings, so she decided to visit him herself and listen to what he had to say and to learn from him.

When Solomon heard that she was coming, he asked the *jinn*,

> *'O chiefs! which of you can bring me her throne before they come to me in submission?' Said an 'Ifrīt of the jinns: 'I will bring it to you before you rise from your council; indeed I have full strength for the purpose, and may be trusted.' Said one who had knowledge of the Book, 'I will bring it to you within the twinkling of an eye!'* (27:38-40)

Solomon wanted to have the throne of the Queen of Sheba waiting for her, so that it would be a lesson for her of the power of God and of the blessings that He bestows upon His prophets. No sooner had

Solomon asked for the throne to be brought, when he saw it before his very eyes. At once he prostrated himself in humble thanks to God for His blessing.

> *'This is by the grace of my Lord! To test me whether I am grateful or ungrateful! And if any is grateful, truly his gratitude is a gain for his own soul; but if any is ungrateful, truly my Lord is Free of all Needs, Supreme in honour!'* (27:40)

Then Solomon ordered that some of the decorations on the throne be changed to see if the Queen would still recognize it.

> *So when she arrived, she was asked, 'Is this your throne?' She said, 'It was just like this.'* (27:42)

The Queen of Sheba recognized her throne, but she failed to understand how it came to be transported to Solomon's palace before she herself had arrived.

The second lesson that Solomon had prepared for the Queen was a palace he had had built upon the sea. The floor of the palace was of transparent crystal glass so that the water was visible beneath, as were the fish and sea plants. When the Queen entered the palace, she did not see the glass and thought that she was going to walk straight into the water, so she raised the hem of her dress to avoid wetting it. Solomon said,

> *'This is but a palace paved smooth with slabs of glass.'* (27:44)

The Queen of Sheba realized that she was in front of the greatest king on earth, and when she heard him speak she understood that he was an equally great prophet. She said,

> *'O my Lord! I have indeed wronged my soul. I do now submit with Solomon to the Lord of the Worlds.'* (27:44)

Solomon lived for many years. Towards the end of his life, he decided to build a temple. While the temple was being built, he would lean on his staff and supervise the work being done by both men and the *jinn*. One day, as he was leaning on his staff, Solomon passed away. He remained, however, leaning on his staff and no-one noticed any difference. When the temple was finished, a small insect ate away at the staff of Solomon, and made him fall over. It was only then that everyone realized that their great prophet had died.

> *Then when We decreed Solomon's death, nothing showed them his death except a little worm of the earth which kept (slowly) gnawing away at his staff.* (34:14)

❖

JOB ﷺ & HIS PATIENCE

Job was a prophet, a descendant of Abraham through his son Isaac. God gave Job everything that people desire on earth. He gave him wisdom and piety, the love and respect of people, much wealth, land and cattle, a large family and many friends. Job was ever-grateful for all the blessings that had been bestowed upon him, and praised God much.

Such humble, sincere and devout worship of God enraged Satan, who tried in every way possible to turn Job away from remembering his Lord. But, no matter how hard he tried, Job remained steadfast in his faith. Not for a moment did he turn away from worshipping God. Satan could not believe that he had managed to lead Adam astray in Paradise and had not been able to succeed with Job. Satan then swore that he would redouble his efforts.

God was well aware of Job's inner strength, for He knows and understands the capabilities of all His creatures. He, therefore, set such tests for Job as might have weakened the faith of other believers, because He knew that Job would withstand the trials with patience and fortitude, and thereby become an example for all generations to come.

God sent Job one trial after another. Within a very short period of time, Job had lost all of his property and had became poor. He then lost his family and friends, and because he had become poor and destitute, many people left him. The trials became even harder when Job suffered a severe illness. His body became very weak, he lost all his strength, and he was in great pain.

As we saw, Satan could not accept his failure to turn Job away from the worship of God. He had interpreted Job's devotion to God as a fear of losing what he possessed if he stopped worshipping God. Satan thought that Job was more attached to his possessions than he was to God Himself. He was, therefore, delighted when Job's circumstances changed to poverty and ill-health, and saw in this his opportunity to finally turn Job away from God. So Satan went to Job and whispered to him, "You were always grateful to God for all the favours He gave you. You used to invoke Him all the time. Now will you still thank Him for all the sufferings He has inflicted upon you?"

Job was deeply angered at Satan's attempt to trick him and to turn him away from the worship of God. At once, in response to Satan's whisperings, he bowed down to the ground before God, thanking Him and seeking His protection. And thus, Job, despite what had befallen him, continued to worship God and to praise Him just as much as he had done when he had been healthy, rich and surrounded by his family and friends.

The only person who had remained with Job was his wife. She took care of him, consoled him and saw to all of his needs. When they had no money left, she went out to work as a servant in order to provide for her husband. But there came a time when she could not even find work, and when there was nothing to eat at home. All that Job's wife had left was her beautiful long hair; and this she did not hesitate to cut off and sell in order to buy food for Job. Job's wife, like Job himself, was extremely patient in spite of all that had happened to them.

When Satan had no success in tempting Job, he turned his attention on Job's wife, and sought to destroy Job through her. As Job's illness became worse, and his anguished wife desperate, Satan would remind her of the luxurious life she had once known, and tried to convince her that Job's illness would never end. Finally, one day, Job's wife was feeling vulnerable, and, in a moment of weakness, she went to her husband and asked him how much longer God's trials would last. "When will God put an end to your suffering?" Angered by Satan's deception, and his wife's yielding to it, Job ordered his wife to leave him at once, saying that he would no longer accept food or drink from her.

Job was now all alone. As his suffering and loneliness worsened, he humbly turned to God, not in complaint but in prayer, saying,

> *'Truly distress has seized me, but You are the Most Merciful of those that are Merciful.'* (21:83)

60

God saw that no trial would turn Job away from worshipping Him, and so He brought Job's trials to an end.

> *We listened to him, We removed the distress that was on him, and We restored his people to him, and doubled their number, as a Grace from Ourselves, and as a reminder for all who serve Us.* (21:84)

God ordered Job to

> *'Strike with your foot, here is water in which to wash, cool and refreshing, and water to drink.'* (38:42)

Job struck the ground as commanded, and a spring of water gushed forth. Job quenched his thirst and bathed the sores that covered his body. No sooner had he done so, when his disease disappeared! He was healed and his body was restored to its former strength.

Meanwhile, Job's wife was beside herself with worry. She could not bear the idea of her husband all alone in his illness. She thought to herself, "I will just go and have a look, from a distance, and see how he is." As Job's wife approached, she saw Job himself coming towards her. To her amazement, he suffered no illness and was in perfect health. Only a few hours ago, she had left him in a most pitiful state, riddled with disease and unable to walk. Now, here he was safe and healthy! Job explained to his wife how God had healed him, and she fell to her knees and bowed her head in gratitude to God for His great mercy.

God's mercy has no bounds. Not only did He cure Job's illness, but He also restored to him his family and friends, and blessed him with even more than he had had before.

> *Then We heard his prayer and removed that distress from which he suffered, and We restored him his household and more with them, a mercy from Ourselves, and a remembrance for the worshippers.* (21:84)

Job's life is an excellent example of piety and patience; and everyone should follow his example when they suffer any loss of health, wealth or of family. God concluded the story of Job as follows,

> *'We found him steadfast, how excellent a slave! He was ever turning in repentance (to his Lord).* (38:44) ❖

JONAH ﷺ & THE WHALE

LIKE JOB, Jonah was a descendant of Abraham through his son Isaac. It is related that Jonah was sent by God as a prophet to the people of Ninevah, a city in the north of present-day Iraq, to summon them to belief in the One God. For many years, Jonah tried hard to guide his people. But they refused to listen to the message he brought, nor would they listen to his warnings of the wrath of God, and the terrible punishment they would suffer if they continued stubbornly to disbelieve. Their only answer was, "We shall not pay heed to your call, nor shall we be frightened by your threats. Indeed, if you speak the truth then bring upon us the punishment you promise." And therefore, in response to his sincere and truthful guidance, Jonah only received curses and ill-treatment from his people.

One day, Jonah's anger was such that he felt he could no longer stand such treatment. Forgetting that his duty was solely to convey the message of God, and that guidance lies ultimately in His Hands, Jonah felt that he had failed. Without asking for permission from God, Jonah decided to leave his people and abandon his mission to them.

No sooner had Jonah left Ninevah, when the city was plunged into darkness. At once, the people of Ninevah realized Jonah had told them the truth, and that the punishment of God was now upon them. Deep remorse at their rejection of Jonah's message now filled their hearts, and they wished that he would return to be with them in their hour of need. All of the city's inhabitants went out in search of Jonah, while at the same time beseeching God to forgive them and to accept their repentance. So sincere were they in their prayers, that God accepted their repentance and ceased to punish them. And so, the people of Ninevah went back to their city hoping that Jonah would return to live among them as their prophet and teacher.

Jonah, meanwhile, had continued to walk until he had reached a port on the sea. Feeling unhappy and sorrowful, he decided to sail to another land and so boarded a ship that was preparing to lift anchor.

The ship sailed for many days, then, one night, when the ship was far away from land, a violent storm broke out. Fierce winds battered the ship and huge waves engulfed it, flooding the decks. The captain was puzzled, for storms never occurred at that time of year. Now, in those days it was believed that a storm out of season was caused by some ill-omened person on board, and so the captain decided to cast lots to find out who that person was. He wrote the names of the passengers on separate pieces of paper, put them in a box, and then drew one out. The name he drew out was that of Jonah. The captain tried once more, and again Jonah's name was drawn. When the same thing happened a third time, Jonah realized that he would have to obey the captain's order and jump into the sea. This, the people believed would save them from the storm.

As he prepared to jump over the side of the ship, Jonah understood that he had done wrong to abandon his people without the permission of God. Looking out at the dark night, full of the roar of wind and waves, he deeply regretted losing his temper. He knew now that he should never have deserted the people to whom God had sent him.

Expecting to drown in the terrible storm, Jonah threw himself over the side. However, no sooner had his body hit the high waves, when a big whale surfaced and swallowed him up whole. Jonah found himself inside the stomach of the whale in total darkness. At first, Jonah thought he had died, but he quickly realized he could move his limbs. In the darkness he prayed silently, and then aloud,

'There is no God save You. Be Glorified! I have been a wrong-doer.'
(21:87)

Over and over again, Jonah repeated this prayer, and as he did so, the whale came to rest on the seabed, for it felt the weight of the words that Jonah was repeating, and understood that the man in its stomach must be a prophet.

God heard Jonah's prayer and saw the sincerity of his repentance. So He commanded the whale to cast Jonah onto the shore. Jonah was now back on dry land. But the time he had spent in the stomach of the whale had made him ill, and he was too weak to move. In His mercy, God made a leafy plant near Jonah grow to a great height, so as to shade him from the hot sun while he recovered his strength.

Once Jonah was well again, God sent him back to his people. And so, Jonah returned to Nineveh, to find that his people had abandoned the worship of idols and now worshipped the One God. Had Jonah not repented sincerely and uttered the words of his prayer, he would have remained inside the whale until the Day of Judgement.

Had it not been that he repented and glorified God, he would certainly have remained inside the fish till the Day of Resurrection. (37:143-144)

ZACHARIAH ﷺ & JOHN ﷺ

OVER THE YEARS, God sent many prophets to the Children of Israel in order to guide them back to the right path and remind them of His favours. But as is the nature of people, they eventually forgot the teachings of their prophets and became distracted by the affairs of the world so that they cared little about religion. Many prophets followed David and Solomon, and one of them was Zachariah.

God had endowed Zachariah with great knowledge and wisdom, and had commanded him to urge his people to follow the right path and to worship God alone. Most of the people were merely concerned with amassing money; only a few remained good and righteous. Zachariah started preaching the message of God. It was his habit to preach during the day and to spend his nights in prayer.

In this way, Zachariah grew old. As his body became weak and his hair turned grey, he began to wonder who would continue his work after his death, for he feared that his people would forget all their religious teachings if there was no-one to guide them. So he prayed to God with all his heart to bless him with a child. Zachariah knew that God was merciful and that He had the power to give without stint to whoever He chooses.

'O my Lord! I have grown old, and the hair on my head has turned grey: yet I have always prospered when I have prayed to You. Now I fear what the people will do after me. My wife is barren, so give me an heir as from You, one that will truly represent me, and represent the descendants of Jacob; and make him, O my Lord! one with whom You are well-pleased!'

(35:4-6)

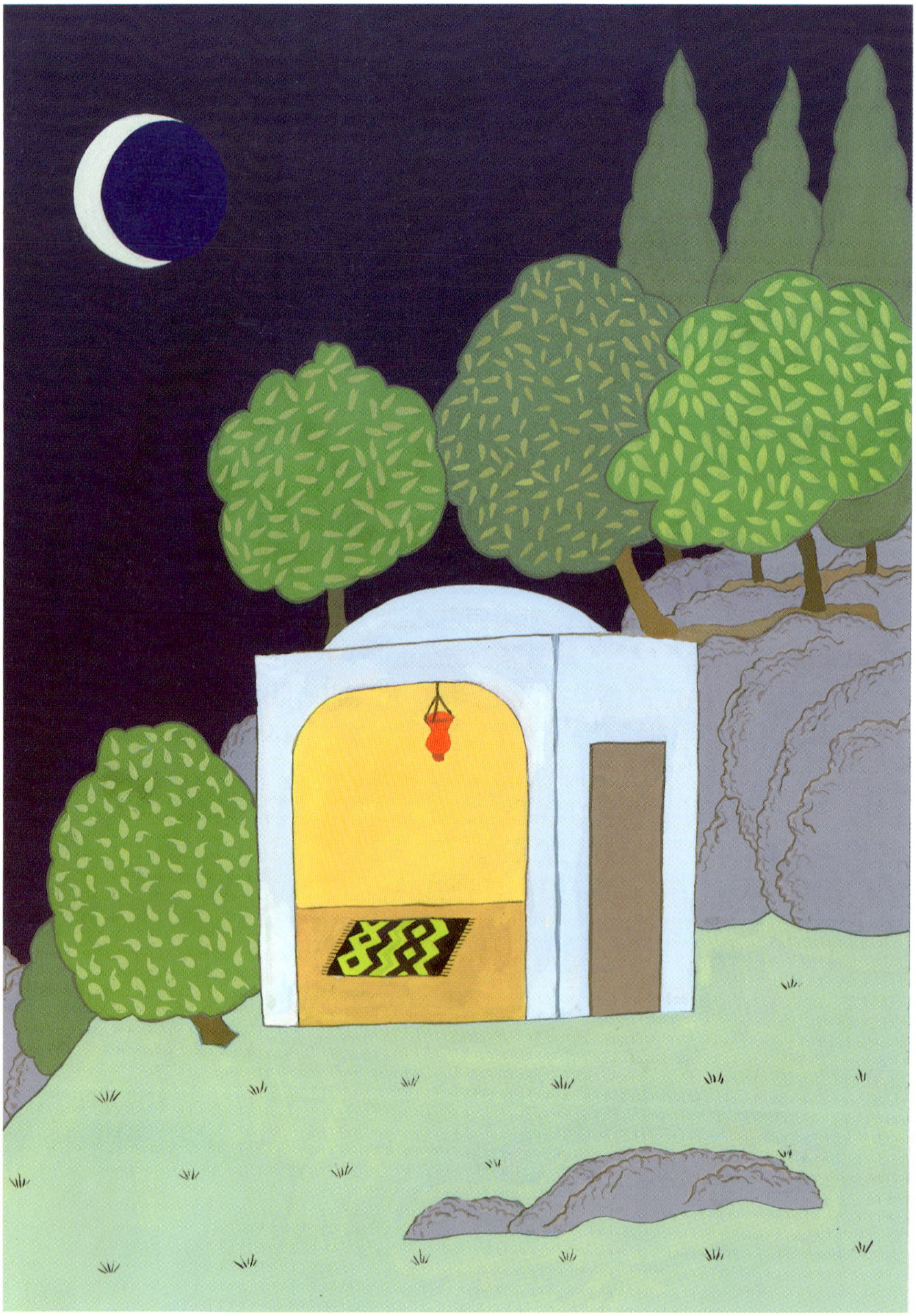

Scarcely had Zachariah finished his prayer, when angels came to him and announced,

> 'God gives you glad tidings of Yaḥyā (John), bearing witness to the Will of God (He will be) noble, chaste and a prophet of the righteous.' (3:39)

Zachariah was overjoyed at the news that he would have a son called John. However, he remained puzzled,

> 'O my Lord! How shall I have a son, seeing I am very old and my wife is barren?' (3:40)

The answer that came to him was,

> So it will be God does what He wills. (3:40)

Zachariah asked God to give him a sign as to when this miracle would happen and God told him that a time would come when he would be unable to speak for three days, though he would suffer no illness.

Zachariah stayed in his prayer-niche, worshipping and invoking God. Then, one day, when he ventured out to his people to see to their affairs as he was wont to do, he found that he was unable to speak. Through sign language he made them understand that they should invoke God morning and evening.

> So Zachariah came out to his people from his prayer-niche; he told them by signs to celebrate God's praises in the morning and in the evening. (19:11)

Zachariah returned to his prayer-niche, grateful to God for His Goodness and happy to await the birth of his son.

When her time came, Zachariah's wife gave birth to a son who God had already named John. God blessed him with many favours which made him different from other children. From an early age, God endowed him with wisdom as well as with knowledge of the Scriptures.

> 'O Yaḥyā! take hold of the Book with might.' And We gave him wisdom even as a youth. (19:12)

John's reading and understanding of the Scriptures, when only a child, surpassed even that of the greatest scholars; and his wisdom and sound judgement were admired by the wisest in the land. Furthermore, God had bestowed a kind nature and a pure heart upon John. John was devoted to his parents, and showed great affection and tenderness towards them. Indeed, John's love embraced everything around him, including the animals and all of nature. Often he would leave his village and stay alone in the wilderness for days, surviving on the plants he gathered. There, in solitude, John would invoke God, and weep incessantly out of love for, and fear of, his Lord. In the Qur'ān, it is said of John,

> *So Peace on him the day he was born, the day that he dies and the day that he will be raised up again!* (19:15)

Like his father Zachariah, John was also a prophet to the Children of Israel. John urged them to believe in God alone, "Pray much, and invoke God frequently!" "Fast and give in charity to the poor!" Such were the pleas of John to his people.

One day, John was summoned to appear before the King who ruled that land. The King had heard about John's wisdom, and wished to ask him for advice. Now, the King had a problem; he wanted to marry a particular woman, but was not certain if such a marriage was permissible or not. To the King's sorrow, John told him that the marriage would not be legal.

On hearing that John had opposed the marriage, the woman who hoped to marry the King was enraged, and decided to get rid of John who was the only obstacle between her and the throne. She was certain of her great influence on the King, and used his love for her to persuade him to kill John.

And so, it came to pass. The King's soldiers searched for John, came upon him as he was in prayer and killed him. Thus was one of God's prophets, the kind and wise John, killed by people who had no regard for the truth and who, blinded by their worldly desires, had forgotten the punishment that their acts would bring upon them both in this life and in the next.

❖

JESUS ﷺ & HIS MIRACLES

ʿIMRĀN WAS A learned and pious man, a descendant of the prophet David, and brother-in-law to the prophet Zachariah. ʿImrān was one of the elders of his people and was held in great respect by them. He was often consulted on difficult matters and his advice always showed great wisdom. Now, ʿImrān and his wife longed for children as they had none. They frequently prayed to God for a child, and ʿImrān's wife promised that if they had a child she would consecrate it to the service of the temple.

ʿImrān's wife became pregnant and with great joy and longing she awaited the birth of her child. When her time came, she gave birth to a beautiful baby girl who she named Mary.

> *When she was delivered, she said, 'O my Lord! Behold! I am delivered of a female child!' And God knew best what she brought forth. 'And no wise is the male like the female. I have named her Mary, and I commend her and her offspring to Your protection from the Evil Satan.'* (3:36)

Mary's mother now had a problem. She had promised God to consecrate her child to the temple, but it was the custom in those days to consecrate only boys to the temple. Mary's mother knew that it was God's choice that her child be a girl, and she waited to see how He would help her to fulfil her promise.

When Mary was still a child her father ʿImrān passed away. At his death, the elders gathered together to discuss who should be Mary's guardian. Although the obvious choice was Zachariah, their prophet and Mary's uncle, they all wanted the honour of being her guardian. They decided to draw lots to determine who the guardian should be. But each time the lots were drawn, Zachariah's name was the one chosen, and so the elders of the tribe agreed that he should have custody of ʿImrān's daughter.

> *Her Lord happily accepted her, and saw that she grew up in His Grace. To the care of Zachariah was she assigned.* (3:37)

After a few years, Zachariah gave the young Mary a special room in the temple to use as a prayer-niche or *miḥrāb*. And so, the promise that Mary's mother had made to God came to be. God had granted Mary this special favour because He had already planned a great future for her; He had chosen her to be an example of purity and piety to all the world.

> *O Mary! God has chosen you and purified you, and chosen you above the women of all the worlds.* (3:42)

In the prayer-niche, Mary worshipped God and performed her religious duties. Mary would spend whole nights in prayer, and soon everyone came to know of her purity and outstanding virtue. Zachariah was the only person to visit Mary when she was in her prayer-niche. To his surprise, he would often find that Mary had food. For example, in the summer, she would have winter fruit and, in the winter, she would have summer fruit. Zachariah could not understand where the food came from, especially as he knew that he was the only person to be allowed into the prayer-niche. One day, Zachariah asked Mary,

> *'O Mary! from where does this come to you?'* (3:37)

Mary's answer was,

> *'From God. God provides for whoever He pleases without measure.'* (3:37)

One day, as Mary was praying in her prayer-niche, God sent the Archangel Gabriel to her.

> *Then We sent to her our angel, and he appeared before her just like a man.* (19:17)

Mary was very frightened to find a man standing in front of her and she said,

> *'I seek refuge from you with God Most Gracious.'* (19:18)

Gabriel informed her that he was not a human being, but only a messenger from God, who had come to bestow upon her a son. This child would be pure and faultless, a miracle to the world, and a great prophet.

> *'O Mary! God gives you glad tidings of a Word from Him; his name will be Christ Jesus, the son of Mary. He will be held in honour in this world and in the Hereafter and will be of the company of those nearest to God.'* (3:45)

Mary was astounded by the news, for she was not married and lived a life of devotion to God.

> *'How shall I have a son, seeing that no man has touched me and I am not unchaste.'* (19:20)

The angel reminded her that God is All-Powerful,

> *'So it will be. Your Lord says, "That is easy for Me. We will make him a sign for all men and a mercy from Us." It is a matter decreed.'* (19:21)

Mary was deeply affected by Gabriel's words, and by the dazzling light radiating from him. And just as he had appeared, Gabriel disappeared. Mary returned to her prayers, her feelings a mixture of joy and amazement. She now remained in the prayer-niche in the temple, leaving it only when absolutely necessary.

As the days passed, Mary was filled with peace and happiness, for God had chosen her above all women with a marvellous miracle. When she felt the first pains of childbirth, Mary left the temple sanctuary and went to a remote place. She had been thinking about what her people would say when they saw her son; she knew that they would not believe that the baby had no father and would make accusations against her even though she lived alone in her prayer-niche. Mary was now in great pain, and as she sat herself under a palm-tree, she said,

> *'Oh! Would that I had died before this! Would that I had been a thing forgotten and out of sight!'* (19:23)

Mary then heard a voice saying,

> *'Grieve not! Your Lord has provided a stream beneath you. Shake towards you the trunk of the palm-tree; it will let fall ripe dates for you. So eat and*

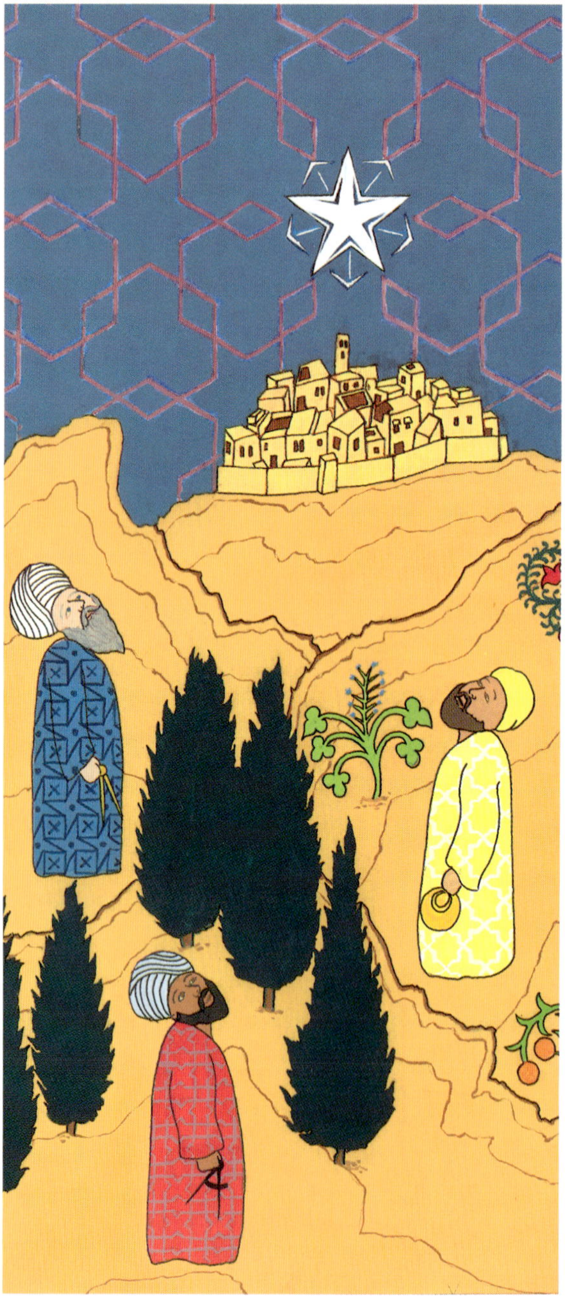

drink, comfort yourself and be glad. And if you see anyone, say, "I have vowed a fast to God Most Gracious, and will speak to no-one today."'

(19:24-6)

Consoled by the voice, Mary gave birth to a son who God had already named Jesus. She then returned home carrying him in her arms. And just as she had feared, her people reproached her and asked her many questions; but she remained silent. When they persisted in their queries, she pointed to the baby. This surprised everyone, and they said,

'How can we talk to one who is a child in the cradle?' (19:29)

It was then that God made baby Jesus perform his first miracle, for the blessed baby spoke and said,

'I am indeed a servant of God. He has given me revelation and made me a prophet. He has made me blessed wherever I may be, and has enjoined on me prayer and charity as long as I live. He has made me kind to my mother; and not overbearing or a sinner. So peace be upon me the day I was born, the day I die, and the day that I shall be raised up again.' (19:30-33)

The people were greatly moved by the infant's words. It was indeed miraculous that he had been born without a father and could speak while still a baby. And thus, the news of Jesus' miraculous birth spread quickly. From far and wide, people came to see the child with their own eyes.

At that time, Palestine, the land in which Jesus was born, was ruled by a very cruel king. Soon news reached the King of Jesus' birth. He grew worried and thought to himself that the coming of a prophet and the gathering of people around him would threaten his power. The King then heard that three wise men had seen the birth of a new star which was now shining in the night-sky over Palestine. They had said that this indicated the birth of a great prophet who would save his people, and they had come to Palestine to pay homage to him. The King became furious and ordered his soldiers to search for the three wise men, as well as for the child and its mother.

Mary was advised to leave Palestine in order to escape from the King. She set off with her son across the Sinai desert to Egypt. Mary and Jesus settled in Egypt until they heard that the wicked King had died. Together they then returned to their home-land.

As he was growing up, Jesus showed signs of great gifts. While playing with his friends, he would tell them what they had eaten that day and what they possessed in their homes without ever having been there. He also showed an exceptional ability for learning. Often he was the only one paying attention in class, and he loved to discuss religious matters with the religious teachers in the temple. In fact, one day, Jesus was so engrossed in discussion at the temple that he forgot to return home at his appointed time. Mary grew anxious, she went out looking for him, but could find him nowhere. He was not at school and he was not with his friends. Finally, Mary went to the temple to ask if anyone had seen her son; and there she found him talking with the rabbis. Jesus was sorry for having made his mother anxious, he had just forgotten the time.

Jesus grew to manhood. He was a model of humility and kindness. He was compassionate with the poor, he fed the hungry and helped the weak. He was exceedingly pious and spent many hours in prayer. Jesus did not settle in any particular town or village, but was constantly moving from one place to another preaching to people about God and about prayer. Wherever he went, he was welcomed by people, both rich and poor, who could see that he was a prophet sent from God. But there were others who refused to believe in Jesus and his message and accused him of lying.

In order to convince people of the truth of his mission, God had given Jesus the ability to perform miracles. Jesus could mould a bird out of clay, breathe on it and the bird would come to life; he was able to give sight to those born blind; he was able to cure lepers; he was even able to raise the dead.

> *'I come to you with a sign from your Lord. I make for you out of clay the figure of a bird, breathe on it, and it becomes a bird by God's leave. I heal those born blind, and the lepers, and I raise the dead, by God's leave. I tell you what you eat and what you store in your houses. Surely in this is a sign for you if you did believe.'* (3:49)

God also gave Jesus disciples who helped him spread his mission. These disciples went everywhere with Jesus. One day they found themselves in a desert and they had no food with them. The disciples asked Jesus,

'Can your Lord send down to us a table set with food from Heaven?'

(5:112)

Jesus was afraid that his disciples had lost their faith in God's power. But the disciples reassured him; they said they wanted to be witnesses to a miracle. So Jesus prayed to God,

'O God our Lord! Send us from Heaven a table with food, that it may be for us a solemn feast and a sign from You.' (5:114)

God answered Jesus,

'I will send it down to you. But if any of you after this does not believe, I shall punish him with a punishment such as I have not inflicted on anyone in all the worlds.' (5:115)

Jesus and his disciples rejoiced and ate of the miracle sent them from Heaven. When they were finished, they gave thanks to God and rose to continue with their travels and their preaching.

Now despite the great goodness of Jesus and of all the miracles that he performed by God's leave, there were people who did not believe in him. They feared that Jesus was gathering too many followers around him, and that no-one would be left to follow them. And so they sought to rid themselves of Jesus. But try as they could, they were unable to find him anywhere. Whenever they thought that they had found out where he was, and that they would be able to capture him, God would warn Jesus and he would move on before they arrived. Jesus' enemies despaired of finding him themselves. So they decided to go to the Governor of Palestine and tell him that Jesus was claiming to be a king and that he was preparing to take the Governor's place in ruling Palestine. They knew that the Governor had many soldiers, and that they would be able to find Jesus. The Governor sent his soldiers out to look for Jesus, and they came upon him with his disciples in a garden. But God protected Jesus, and raised him to Heaven before anyone could capture or harm him. And so, Jesus' last days on earth were just as miraculous as his first.

God raised him up to Him, and God is exalted in power, Wise. (4:158)

❖

بِسْمِ اللَّهِ الرَّحْمَٰنِ الرَّحِيمِ

اقْرَأْ بِاسْمِ رَبِّكَ الَّذِي خَلَقَ ۞ خَلَقَ الْإِنسَانَ مِنْ عَلَقٍ ۞ اقْرَأْ وَرَبُّكَ الْأَكْرَمُ ۞ الَّذِي عَلَّمَ بِالْقَلَمِ ۞ عَلَّمَ الْإِنسَانَ مَا لَمْ يَعْلَمْ ۞ كَلَّا إِنَّ الْإِنسَانَ لَيَطْغَىٰ ۞ أَن رَّآهُ اسْتَغْنَىٰ ۞ إِنَّ إِلَىٰ رَبِّكَ الرُّجْعَىٰ ۞ أَرَأَيْتَ الَّذِي يَنْهَىٰ ۞ عَبْدًا إِذَا صَلَّىٰ ۞ أَرَأَيْتَ إِن كَانَ عَلَى الْهُدَىٰ ۞ أَوْ أَمَرَ بِالتَّقْوَىٰ ۞ أَرَأَيْتَ إِن كَذَّبَ وَتَوَلَّىٰ ۞ أَلَمْ يَعْلَم بِأَنَّ اللَّهَ يَرَىٰ ۞ كَلَّا لَئِن لَّمْ يَنتَهِ لَنَسْفَعًا بِالنَّاصِيَةِ ۞ نَاصِيَةٍ كَاذِبَةٍ خَاطِئَةٍ ۞ فَلْيَدْعُ نَادِيَهُ ۞ سَنَدْعُ الزَّبَانِيَةَ ۞ كَلَّا لَا تُطِعْهُ وَاسْجُدْ وَاقْتَرِب ۞

MUḤAMMAD ﷺ THE FINAL PROPHET

ACCORDING TO THE Qur'ān, the last prophet to be sent to mankind by God was Muḥammad. Muḥammad was a descendant of Abraham through his son Ishmael. We have seen how together, Abraham and Ishmael, had built the Kaʿba. Ishmael had then chosen to live close to the Kaʿba, summoning people to the worship of the One God. Within a short space of time, the land he lived in became a stopping place for merchant caravans on their way north, and eventually it grew into a flourishing city known by the name of Mecca.

The descendants of Ishmael became tribes and spread out across the Arabian peninsula. Some of his descendants, however, had remained in Mecca and were known as the tribe of Quraysh. With the passing of the years, the people of Mecca turned away from the truth that Abraham and Ishmael had once taught. They started worshipping idols which they placed around the Kaʿba. The other Arab tribes, however, still travelled from all over the peninsula in order to visit the Kaʿba and to perform the pilgrimage (*Ḥajj*).

One of the elders of the tribe of Quraysh was a man called Qusayy, and to him fell the honour of taking charge of the Kaʿba, of showing hospitality to the pilgrims and of giving them food and drink. Qusayy's function was passed down to his sons until it reached his great-grandson ʿAbd al-Muṭṭalib. ʿAbd al-Muṭṭalib had a son by the name of ʿAbd Allāh whom he loved greatly. When ʿAbd Allāh reached the age of manhood, his father chose Āmina bint Wahb to be his wife. Āmina was a most excellent girl of Quraysh and ʿAbd Allāh one of the finest young men of the tribe.

The wedding took place, and ʿAbd Allāh spent a number of months with his wife. Then he left with a merchant caravan for the north. On the return journey, however, he was taken ill and decided to remain behind in Yathrib, a city north of Mecca, until he recovered. But his condition worsened, and shortly afterwards he died.

Āmina was deeply sorrowed by the loss of her husband. She also feared for the child she was carrying, a child destined never to see its father. Yet it was the wisdom of God that this very child should grow up to be a prophet.

The time for Āmina's child to be born drew near. Although her heart was filled with sadness, she always felt a great sense of calm, for she had seen in a dream that she would be blessed with a son who would one day be great, and that his name would be Muḥammad.

The child was born, and news of the birth reached ʿAbd al-Muṭṭalib, as he was sitting beside the Kaʿba. He rejoiced greatly at the birth of his grandson, and began to think of a name for him. Six days passed and still he could not decide what it should be. Then, on the seventh night, he had a dream in which an invisible speaker commanded him to name the child Muḥammad, as Āmina had already dreamt.

ʿAbd al-Muṭṭalib called the elders of Mecca to a gathering, and announced the name of the child. It was a name strange to the Arabs. When ʿAbd al-Muṭṭalib was asked why he had not chosen a name with which they were all familiar, he replied, "I wish him to be praised (*maḥmūd*, from the same root-word as Muḥammad) both by God in the heavens and by people on the earth." Thus the birth of the prophet Muḥammad was enfolded both in his mother's tenderness and his grandfather's loving care.

In time, Āmina decided to send her son to the desert where the climate was better than in Mecca. Quraysh were accustomed to doing this in order to preserve the health of their children. The young Muḥammad travelled in the care of a Bedouin woman named Ḥalīma. Ḥalīma was a poor woman of delicate health with a son of her own to feed; but no sooner did she return to her home in the desert, carrying with her this precious child, when much good fortune rained down upon her and continued to do so for as long as the child remained in her care.

When Muḥammad was approaching his sixth year, his mother took him to visit one of his uncles in Yathrib. Muḥammad spent a happy time with his cousins. But on the journey back to Mecca, Āmina fell ill and died.

Sadly Muḥammad returned to Mecca accompanied by his mother's maid.

ʿAbd al-Muṭṭalib now became the child's legal guardian. He looked after him with very special care, favouring him over all his other cousins, and keeping him always at his side. A sign of this favour could be seen when ʿAbd al-Muṭṭalib would receive tribal elders. He would sit on a carpet by the Kaʿba and only Muḥammad would be allowed to sit there beside him.

Unfortunately, two years after the death of Āmina, ʿAbd al-Muṭṭalib passed away. The child was now adopted by his uncle Abū Ṭālib. Abū Ṭālib was a man with many children, but it was not long before Muḥammad became like a son to him.

Once, when Quraysh were making a trip to Syria, Abū Ṭālib decided to take his nephew Muḥammad along with him. The caravan happened to halt at a place near to the cell of a certain monk named Baḥīra. Caravans would often pass that way. Yet, on this particular occasion, the monk came out to inspect the new arrivals, for his curiosity had been aroused by a wondrous sight. He had noticed a single raincloud sheltering the caravan all throughout its journey. Then, suddenly he saw it disappear as one of the members of the party moved off to sit beneath a tree.

Now, Baḥīra knew, from his reading of the scriptures, that a prophet was expected after Jesus; he also knew that the time for his coming was at hand. He sensed something extraordinary about this caravan, and so he sent word inviting the party to come and take refreshments with him.

One by one, he began to examine them until finally his gaze fell upon Muḥammad. Watching him carefully all the while, he took him aside and asked questions to which Muḥammad replied. Finally, before the caravan went on its way, Baḥīra urged Abū Ṭālib to take good care of his nephew Muḥammad and to be sure to always guard him well.

Muḥammad grew to be a young man of good character. He was so honest and truthful that people called him the Trustworthy (*al-Amīn*). He loved to be alone, and would often leave the city to shepherd the flocks and contemplate the wonders of nature.

At the age of twenty-five, Muḥammad married Khadīja, a wealthy noblewoman of Quraysh. Before this, he had traded abroad on her behalf, and although he was considerably younger that she, he had greatly impressed her with his good character and trustworthy nature. Together they lived in peace and happiness. They had four daughters, Zaynab, Ruqayya, Umm Kulthūm and Fāṭima, and also two little boys, who sadly died while still infants.

While Quraysh worshipped idols, Muḥammad woshipped God alone. Muḥammad hated to see idols inside the Kaʿba for he knew that his ancestors, Abraham and Ishmael, had built it as a place for the worship of the One God. Muḥammad would often journey far out of Mecca, away from its people and the idols, and take shelter in a cave at Mount Ḥirā'. There he devoted himself to worshipping God. He pondered the universe and its Creator, and would think about how far his people had gone astray. Sometimes, these periods alone in the cave would endure for many long days and nights, especially in the month of Ramaḍān. Then he returned home only to take the sparsest supplies of food and drink.

Fifteen years had passed since the marriage of Muḥammad and Khadīja, and Muḥammad was now forty years old. In the Ramaḍān of his fortieth year, Muḥammad made his way as usual to the cave of Mount Ḥirā' intending to spend the month of Ramaḍān there in prayer. During one of the last ten nights of the month, whilst he was in deepest thought, the Archangel Gabriel suddenly appeared before him. Gabriel said to him, "Read!" Astonished and deeply stirred, Muḥammad replied, "I am not one who reads." At this the Archangel embraced him tightly, then released him and repeated his demand. Muḥammad gave the same reply. So Gabriel did as he had done before, and for a third time commanded him to read. Once more, Muḥammad repeated, "I am not one who reads." Then the Archangel lifted up his voice saying,

'Read in the name of your Lord who created.' (96:1)

This verse from God marked the beginning of Muḥammad's mission to mankind. Throughout his life, he would receive many other verses which together make up the Holy Book of Islam, the Qur'ān.

The Archangel disappeared just as suddenly as he had appeared, and Muḥammad was left all alone in the cave. Overwhelmed and deeply awed by what had just happened. Muḥammad hurriedly left the cave, and made for his home in Mecca. But he was not far from the cave, when he heard a voice from above him saying, "O Muḥammad! You are the Messenger of God, and I am the angel Gabriel." Muḥammad looked up at the sky and, wherever he looked, there was the Archangel Gabriel.

Exhausted he returned to his house, his body shaking as if with fever. He requested his wife Khadīja to cover him with a cloak or blanket. This she did, watching him with tender concern.

When he felt more in control of himself, Muḥammad related to Khadīja what had happened with the Archangel, and recited to her the verse that Gabriel had taught him. Khadīja then left Muḥammad to rest and went to see a cousin of hers, a learned and pious man, whose name was Waraqa bin Nawfal.

Waraqa had studied the holy books. He had read the Gospel and had become a Christian. Khadīja related to him all that Muḥammad had told her. Waraqa listened with the greatest interest. When Khadīja had finished, he declared to her that Muḥammad would be the prophet of his people, and that Gabriel had come to him bringing a message from the Lord, just as he had done with Moses and Jesus before. Then he confided in his cousin, that he feared for Muḥammad, for no messenger was ever sent to mankind but suffered hardship for preaching the message of God.

After that first night, Gabriel appeared to Muḥammad again and again reciting verse after verse of the Holy Qur'ān. These Muḥammad repeated and memorised with the greatest care.

Muḥammad made ready to deliver the message of God to his closest and most intimate companions. Khadīja was the very first person to believe in his mission. The first boy to convert was ʿAlī, the son of his uncle, Abū Ṭālib. ʿAlī was Muḥammad's constant companion and had become a member of his household. Next, Abū Bakr, an elder of Quraysh and a wealthy merchant was converted.

Soon there was a small group who followed Muḥammad. They used to meet secretly in one or another of their houses, or else they would go out of the city into the desert so that Muḥammad could teach them the worship of the One God.

After a time, Gabriel brought Muḥammad a command from God to start preaching the message publicly to people in Mecca and to the other tribes in the Arabian peninsula. So gathering the Meccans all together, Muḥammad told them that God had chosen him as their prophet. He told them that they must stop worshipping idols and return to worshipping God alone just as their ancestors Abraham and Ishmael had done. Finally, he advised them to obey God's Word, and warned them that God would punish them if they were to disobey.

Upon hearing what Muḥammad had to say, the crowd was, at first, dumbstruck. Certainly they knew him well. They knew of his honesty, of his piety and goodness. Yet, what was this he was now asking them to do? Muḥammad informed them that he was simply a messenger conveying the message of God. He only wanted their salvation and nothing else. At this, the crowd erupted against him. Laughing and jeering they asked him how he expected them to abandon the ways of their fathers?

When the elders of Quraysh realized how determined Muḥammad was to preach his message, they tried all sorts of ways to stop him. They attempted to bribe him with wealth and power. When this failed, they went to his uncle, Abū Ṭālib, and begged him to prevent his nephew from preaching his message and from speaking ill of their idols. Muḥammad paid no heed to all the attempts to hinder him; and Abū Ṭālib did not cease to protect his nephew.

Deeply disturbed at the growing success of Muḥammad's activities, Quraysh were at a loss as to what to do next. Finally, all the elders met together and decided to boycott the Muslims, as the followers of Muḥammad had come to be known, and to refuse to do business with them. Nothing was to be sold to the Muslims and nothing was to be bought from them. There were to be no relations whatsoever with the Muslims. They were even to be denied food and drink. To this effect, the leaders of Quraysh drew up a special document and hung it upon the Kaʿba.

For three years, this boycott of Muḥammad and his followers, continued. During this time the Muslims suffered terrible hardship. Yet, they bore their suffering patiently and did not abandon their religion. At the end of three years, Quraysh realised that their plan had failed and they ceased boycotting the Muslims. They went to take the document off the Kaʿba, but to their amazement they found that it had been eaten up by insects. Sadly, the end of the boycott had come too late for Khadīja; she had fallen ill and soon after died. Not long after her death, the Prophet's uncle, Abū Ṭālib also passed away. With the death of these two people, Muḥammad lost both his beloved wife, and the care and protection of his uncle.

But God was not about to abandon His prophet. One night, as Muḥammad was lying down to sleep, Gabriel suddenly appeared before him. He led him outside where a white steed was waiting. Muḥammad mounted the steed and, together with Gabriel, soared high into the sky. They travelled for some time before coming down in the holy city of Jerusalem. There, Muḥammad found Abraham, Moses, Jesus and a host of other prophets. Muḥammad led them in prayer, then was told by Gabriel that they must continue their journey.

> *Glory be to God Who did take His servant for a journey by night, from the Sacred Mosque to the Furthest Mosque (Jerusalem) whose precincts We did bless, in order that We might show him some of Our signs.* (17:1)

High into the skies they ascended, moving through the heavens one upon the other. At last, they reached the proximity of God. God revealed certain verses of the Holy Qur'ān to Muḥammad, as well as the five daily prayers or *ṣalāt*. Gabriel then guided Muḥammad back through the heavens to Jerusalem and then to Mecca. This event in the life of Muḥammad is called the Isrā' and the Miʿrāj; it was a great consolation to him for all the suffering he had undergone and a tremendous confirmation of his prophethood.

We saw earlier how Muḥammad as a child had visited the city of Yathrib with his mother. Yathrib was a wealthy city, and in it lived two important tribes, the Aws and the Khazraj. A certain number of Jewish tribes also lived in Yathrib. They were people with a holy book, fiercely proud of their religion, and would boast to the Arabs of their knowledge and learning. Their religious leaders, the rabbis, preached the coming of a new prophet, though they believed that he would be a member of their community.

Now at a certain time each year, the Arab tribes would come in large numbers from all over the Peninsula to Mecca in order to perform the pilgrimage and to visit the Kaʿba. News of the teachings of Muḥammad reached the city of Yathrib through a number of returning pilgrims. And so it was, that a party from the tribe of Khazraj decided to make the journey to Mecca to see and hear Muḥammad for themselves. All the while, they had in mind the stories that the Jews of Yathrib used to tell about the coming of a new prophet.

This group met with Muḥammad, listened to what he had to say and were convinced that his mission was true. When they returned home, they related to their kinsmen all that they had been told and many who heard them were persuaded of the truth of Muḥammad's mission.

The following year, more than seventy men left Yathrib and journeyed to Mecca. They met Muḥammad in secret, outside the city, and pledged themselves to protect and defend him should he chose to come and live with them in Yathrib. This the Prophet decided to do. The oath which the men of Yathrib took became known as the Treaty of ʿAqaba. It was the very first treaty in Islam, the name given to the new religion.

> *God was well pleased with the believers when they swore allegiance to you under the tree. He knew what was in their hearts and He sent down tranquility to them and He rewarded them with a speedy victory.* (48:18)

Muḥammad returned to Mecca and urged his followers to leave for Yathrib where they would be free to practice their religion. Those Muslims who were able to travel took this opportunity and, one by one or in groups, stole away from Mecca and from Quraysh who had been ill-treating them for so many years.

When Quraysh discovered that many of the Muslims had escaped, they feared that the Muslims would turn people against them, and that people would no longer come to visit the Kaʿba. Quraysh's wealth depended on the pilgrims who came every year to perform the pilgrimage. Knowing that Muḥammad must surely intend to follow those who had already fled, Quraysh now resolved to kill him. One night, a group of them surrounded Muḥammad's house waiting for the right moment to enter and kill him.

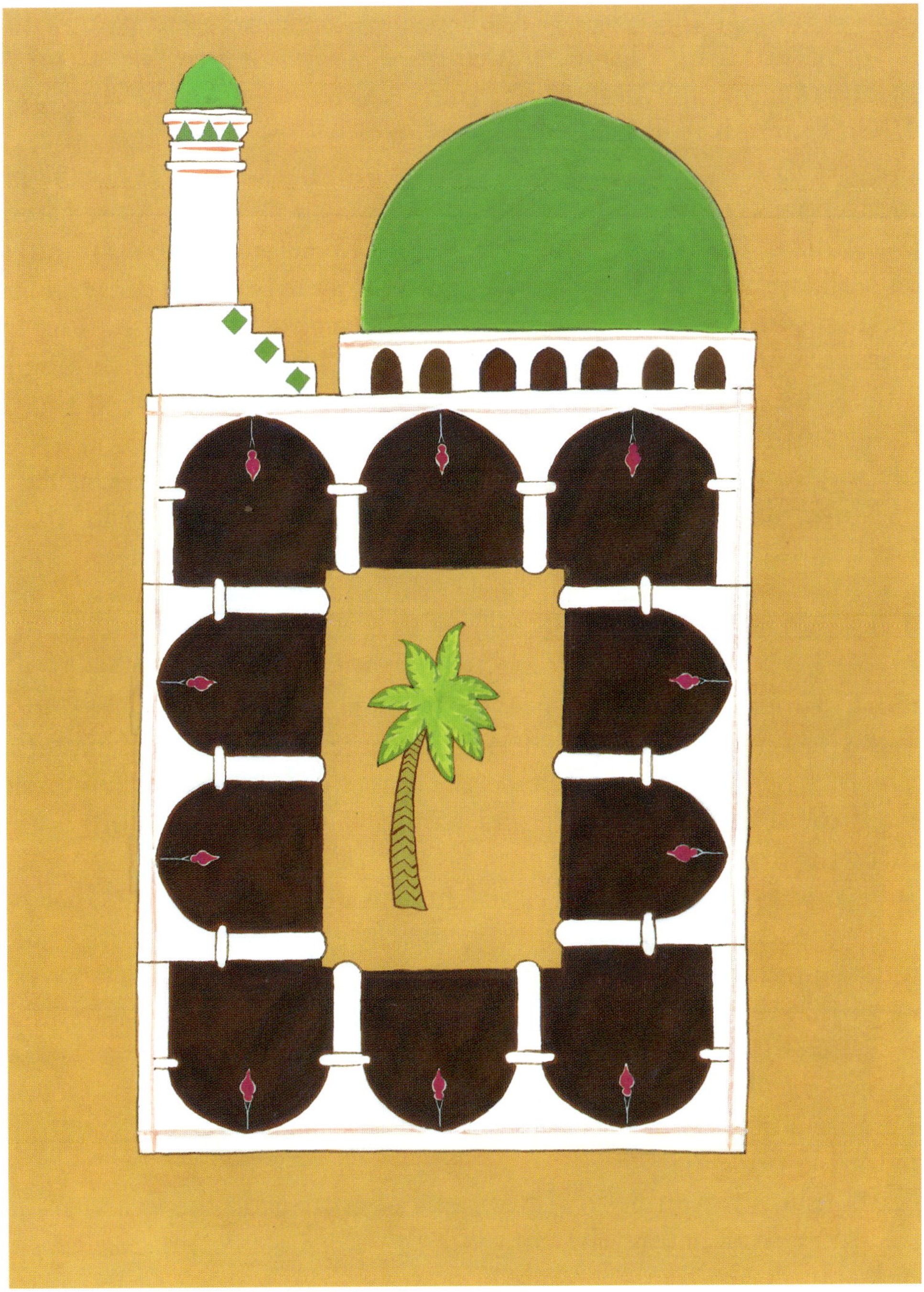

But, God blinded Quraysh and Muḥammad was able to slip away without them ever seeing him leave. Muḥammad was joined by his friend Abū Bakr, and together they left for Yathrib.

When Quraysh realized that Muḥammad had escaped them, they sent out parties to search for him and to bring him back to Mecca. One party found the tracks of Muḥammad and Abū Bakr and were about to catch up with them, but God guided His prophet to a cave in the side of a mountain. After Muḥammad and Abū Bakr had entered, a bird quickly came and built a nest just outside the cave and a spider spun a web across the cave entrance. The party from Quraysh came up to the cave, but, seeing the nesting bird and the spider's web, thought that no-one could have entered the cave without disturbing these two; they decided that Muḥammad could not be inside and so went to look for him elsewhere. When the search-party was gone Muḥammad and Abū Bakr were able to continue on to Yathrib.

The flight of Muḥammad to Yathrib became known as the *Hijra*, and the year it took place became year one of the Muslim calendar. Muḥammad settled down to live in Yathrib, which became known as the City of the Messenger of God, in Arabic Madīnat Rasūl Allāh, or simply the City, Madīna. A mosque was built in which Muḥammad could meet with the Muslims for prayer. He settled what disputes there were between the inhabitants of Madīna, and made an agreement with the Jews which allowed them to live in peace and harmony with the Muslims and still abide by their own religion.

But Quraysh would not leave the Muslims in peace, and over a period of several years the Muslims had to go to battle a number of times against Quraysh and their allies. But, finally, the Muslims grew in number to such a degree that Quraysh were obliged to sign a peace treaty with them. This treaty stated that all hostilities between the two sides should cease, and that the peace should remain unbroken for ten years. The Muslims were also granted free movement in Mecca for three days each year in order to perform the pilgrimage.

The Muslims were able to perform the pilgrimage in the first year of the peace treaty. But before the time for the second pilgrimage had come round, they heard that Quraysh had broken the terms of the treaty by attacking a tribe that was allied to the Muslims. Muḥammad immediately gathered together an army of ten thousand men and marched on Mecca. When the Meccans saw such a huge Muslim army coming over the hills around Mecca they were overwhelmed by fear. Muḥammad then sent word to the Meccans that if they did not fight against him and the Muslims but remained in their homes, their lives would be spared. The Meccans agreed. Muḥammad entered Mecca victorious and made directly for the Kaʿba. There he knelt in grateful prayer to God, and circled around the Holy House with the Muslims following close behind him.

After performing the rites, Muḥammad ordered the destruction of the idols that surrounded the Kaʿba. Thus once more the Kaʿba was restored to its proper role, as it had been when Abraham first built it, namely, a place for the worship of God alone.

> *And say, 'The Truth has arrived, and falsehood has perished; for falsehood is (by its nature) bound to perish.'* (17:81)

The people of Mecca then came to Muḥammad to declare their acceptance of Islam. Fearfully, they wondered what he would do to them. But Muḥammad treated them with kindness and pardoned them for all they had done.

Muḥammad decided not to remain in Mecca but to return to Madīna. He preferred to go back with those people who had been his loyal helpers throughout his mission. The people of Madīna, known as the *Anṣār* or Helpers, were overjoyed at this decision for they had feared that Muḥammad would remain in Mecca, the city of his birth.

Now, when the time for the pilgrimage came round again, Muḥammad set off on his camel for Mecca and with him went a throng of thirty thousand pilgrims. Those who had become Muslims in the early days now thought back to how they had fled, in ones and twos, from the tyranny of Quraysh. By the grace of God, they were returning to Mecca, a mighty host, no longer afraid or persecuted.

Once again, Muḥammad made directly for the Kaʿba and circled around it seven times, the Muslims following in his footsteps. Then he led them just outside Mecca to the mountain at ʿArafa, where they were to spend the day. Here, Muḥammad gave his Farewell Sermon. In it he counselled the Muslims to hold fast to the Book of God, the Qurʾān, and to follow his example, for in the two lay the way to salvation. He instructed them to abandon what they used to practice before the coming of Islam. Lastly, he recited a verse from the Qurʾān,

> *This day I have perfected your religion for you and completed my favour onto you and have chosen for you Islam as a religion.* (5:3)

Many Muslims wept when they heard these words from the Qurʾān, for they understood that if the Prophet's message on earth was complete, then the time of his death must certainly be near at hand.

Back in Madīna, Muḥammad began to feel weak and faint. He, nonetheless, continued to lead the Muslims in prayer. But he soon came down with a fever and Abū Bakr, his old friend and companion, was asked to lead the Muslims in prayer in place of Muḥammad.

A few days into his illness, Muḥammad appeared at the mosque while the prayers were in progress. The Muslims were overjoyed to see him, and Abū Bakr stepped back for Muḥammad to take his place. But Muḥammad signalled for him to continue, and himself prayed sitting by Abū Bakr's side.

Afterward, Muḥammad returned to the house of his wife ʿĀʾisha. There he lay with his head on her lap, half asleep. Suddenly, ʿĀʾisha heard him utter faintly the Qurʾānic verse,

> *With those upon whom God has showered His Favour, the prophets and the saints and the martyrs and the good, and they are the best of companions.*
> (4:69)

From this ʿĀʾisha understood that Muḥammad had chosen to remain no longer on earth, but to return to his Maker. And so the Prophet of Islam peacefully passed away having fulfilled his mission to the end.

❖